BEASTMAKING

A FINGERS-FIRST
APPROACH TO
BECOMING
A BETTER
CLIMBER

BEASTMAKING

NED FEEHALLY

Vertebrate Publishing, Sheffield
www.v-publishing.co.uk

BEASTMAKING

NED FEEHALLY

First published in 2021 by Vertebrate Publishing. Reprinted in 2021.

Vertebrate Publishing, Omega Court, 352 Cemetery Road,
Sheffield S11 8FT, United Kingdom.
www.v-publishing.co.uk

A CIP catalogue record for this book is available from the British Library.

ISBN 978-1-83981-009-1 (Paperback)
ISBN 978-1-83981-010-7 (Ebook)

10 9 8 7 6 5 4 3 2

Front cover © *Nick Brown.*
Back cover The author on *Dandelion Mind*, Badger Cove, England. © *Martin Smith.*
Inside front cover © *Nick Brown.*
Inside back cover The author on the first ascent of *C'est un Alien*,
Rocher Cailleau, Fontainebleau, France. © *John Coefield.*

Photography by Nick Brown unless otherwise credited.
Anatomy illustrations by Ilija Visnjic.

Design and production by Jane Beagley, Vertebrate Publishing.
www.v-publishing.co.uk

Printed in the UK by Severnprint Ltd, a carbon neutral printer.

Printed on FSC Mix Credit certified paper.

Vertebrate Publishing is committed to printing on paper from sustainable sources.

FOREWORD

The exponential rate at which our sport has grown is hard to comprehend. The past decade alone has seen grade boundaries shattered, the emergence of countless prodigies, the birth of dedicated elite training facilities and the introduction of climbing as an Olympic sport. Most outrageously, though, climbing has become cool – I mean, no one saw that coming!

The growth of climbing has seen many people look to the professionals for answers to the question of how to get better. Who doesn't want to know what the secret is? So, where are the famous coaches, who is doing all the research and where can you buy the best training programme ... ?

However, our sport is about so much more than spreadsheets and numbers. It transcends the boundaries between traditional sport and action sport. It's a sport that at any level combines performance and style while requiring composure and resilience.

It seems as though we are at a point where the science and the research are trying to catch up, with a multitude of studies and data trying to categorise inexplicable levels of ability that simply do not come down to basic levels of strength or endurance. Climbing is as much an art form as it is a matter of physical ability.

That being said, most of us can certainly benefit from more understanding of how to train and what to train in order to become stronger. The getting better bit is a little more complicated.

Ned has spent the last 20 years exploring his fascination with the intricate details of what makes elite climbers good and how they get to the top of the sport. His obsessive tendencies have ensured he's not only tried and tested pretty much everything he's learnt, but he's also (very neatly) documented everything. Ned is practical; he's pragmatic and is a self-proclaimed geek when it comes to training.

Read this book with the desire to improve, the dedication to action what you learn and the belief that you can achieve your goals.

Shauna Coxsey

INTRODUCTION

If you've picked up this book you are probably interested in improving your climbing, and you're willing to put some effort into doing just that.

Great, you're in the right place.

It seems as if climbers are always looking for a shortcut to improving. They might pay a coach in the hope that this will automatically make them better, or they might buy an online training programme which has convinced them that it will add a few grades to their climbing. Similarly, they might be happy to buy a fingerboard – and maybe even put it up in their house – before realising that thinking about and actually training on it takes some effort, and the benefits of simply owning a fingerboard are fairly limited.

However, some people are *really* keen to improve, but struggle to know exactly how they should go about it, and even where they should start.

The idea of this book is to provide you with enough information so that you can work out what you need to train, and to help you to train it, but without things being data and jargon dense and too much of a chore to trawl through. I hope that it will give you some new ideas, fresh knowledge and inspiration for your training.

But, just so we are clear from the beginning: there is no shortcut to improving! You'll not find a magic formula in this book. It simply doesn't exist.

While there is an increasing amount of science and data-driven training information out there, climbing is a relatively young sport. The amount of scientific studies into climbing is still very limited. It feels like we're at the stage where the science that's getting done is simply backing up what we have been crowdsourcing in the climbing scene for the past 40 years!

When it comes to writing, filling up a book with citations might make me look clever, but, let's face it, most of you aren't going to be interested in reading up behind the scenes. While I personally find the data-heavy training information out there quite interesting, I appreciate that not everyone is into this. If you're looking for hard facts, science and references then I encourage you to do some extra reading. My experience is that most climbers either just want to know what is best for them to do, or they just need some inspiration and a place to start – they aren't fussed about reading all about the nitty-gritty and specifics of the training protocols. So, rather than diving headlong into the science, I have filtered what I have read and actioned over the years and extracted the most useful and usable nuggets of information to pass on to you as simply as I can.

I have been lucky to have climbed and trained with some of the best climbers in the world. I am both passionate and endlessly fascinated by training and improving. I am always on the lookout for ideas and new information. I like to think I'm not nagging people the whole time, but I do try to absorb as much information as I can when I climb and train with others.

There is a great diversity of strengths and weaknesses among top-end climbers which I find particularly intriguing. Everybody is different and everybody has a slightly different approach to training and trying to improve. Ultimately, the best climbers are those with the right mentality and mindset, not necessarily those who are physically the strongest. Improving our proficiency at climbing seems to be about aggregating marginal gains and ironing out weaknesses across the whole spectrum of climbing ability, as much as it is about doing more pull-ups or hanging off a smaller hold than anyone else.

Everything in this book is based on my personal experience – and long-winded discussions with others who know what they're talking about – and it highlights what has worked for me (and the people I know) over the years. I hope it works for you too.

When it comes to training, there isn't a right or wrong answer. Everybody is different. You are your own experiment.

A BIT MORE ABOUT ME

I wouldn't describe myself as a talented climber. I started when I was nine years old, but it probably wasn't until I was 16 that I got heavily into climbing, and started training for it and taking it seriously. And it wasn't until I was about 26 that I actually began to feel strong and started climbing at a level which I felt was pretty good.

The point I'm trying to make is that I don't think I have a huge amount of natural talent for climbing. I am not physically the strongest, most flexible, fittest or most technically gifted climber out there. However, over the years I have thought a lot, trained a lot, made small steps of progress and have occasionally managed to climb up some rocks and get a few decent competition results along the way.

I think that my strongest attribute is my ability to organise my training and really push myself hard. Although it never feels like hard work, I was – and still am – constantly driven to do things which I think will benefit my climbing and contribute to my goal of wanting to

THE AUTHOR ON *THE ACE*, STANAGE, ENGLAND. © *NICK BROWN*

SHAUNA COXSEY COMPETING AT THE 2019 IFSC CLIMBING WORLD CHAMPIONSHIPS IN HACHIOJI, JAPAN. © *BAND OF BIRDS*

become a well-rounded boulderer. I think this is definitely more of a mental strength than a physical one. I'm also not one to follow the crowd. If I think a training method or approach is useful, I'll go for it, regardless of how daft everyone else thinks it might be.

The result of this is that I have slowly become stronger and more technically able over the years and have achieved way more on rock than I ever would have dreamed as a youngster. I'm not claiming that anyone can become the next Adam Ondra through training, but I do think that everyone is capable of getting to a fairly decent standard with a bit – or a lot! – of work. The real trick is to play the long game. You'll not improve instantly. But if you enjoy what you're doing, then over the years you're bound to see steady improvement.

Throughout this book I'll try to add to my personal experience with examples from someone who I know pretty well who is smaller and lighter than me and who has naturally very strong fingers and almost flawless technique.

Since Shauna and I are married, I should say how wonderful, kind, generous and amazing she is, and how I'm proud of her and that she makes me a better person. Fortunately, though, for the purposes of this book I can simply say that she is one of the best climbers in the world and leave it at that. Phew. Shauna has climbed for over two decades. She has mostly focused on competition climbing and has won 11 bouldering world cups (winning the overall twice), qualified for the Olympic Games and has bouldered Font 8b+ on rock – possibly the second woman in the world to do so. She's mentally very tough and stubborn (lucky me) and she trains incredibly hard.

While I'm sure she's my biggest fan, writing this book has made it quite clear that she is also my harshest critic!

ACKNOWLEDGEMENTS

Massive thanks to everyone who has helped out with this project. Special thanks to:

Paul Houghoughi for loads of ideas, intricate discussions about anatomy and injuries, and endless positivity throughout.

Stu Littlefair for his infinite wisdom and generosity in helping with the endurance chapter.

Will Abbott for helping me to focus some distinctly pixelated concepts at the very beginning.

Jerry Moffatt for input on the history section as well as much encouragement when I was in the thick of banging my head on the keyboard.

Dan Varian, Dave Bowering and Elsie Butler for making 'working' at Beastmaker the most fun job in the world.

Nick Brown for many years of brilliant photography, but especially for all his help and hard work during this project.

Martin Smith for sneaking some great photos during many fun sessions over the years.

Gracie Martin and Kieran Mercer for being willing and tolerant models and baking plenty of cakes to keep me going.

The Climbing Hangar and the Depot climbing walls for letting us invade their fantastic facilities to take photos.

John Coefield for making it all happen. And Jane Beagley for the incredible design.

Mum and Dad for many things, and also for making me think that writing a book was a totally normal thing to attempt.

Shauna for everything.

JAMES BLAY ON *GREAT WHITE*, CURBAR EDGE, ENGLAND. © *NICK BROWN*

TRAINING: THE BASICS

WHY TRAIN?

Have you ever stopped to think about what you want to get out of climbing?

Do you just enjoy going climbing? Do you want to generally improve? Become a very well-rounded climber? Do you want to train for one particular boulder problem or route? Or a trip? Do you want to win an Olympic medal? Do you want to free El Cap? Or do you just really want to be able to do a one-arm pull-up? Maybe you just love training.

All of these goals are totally valid, as is every goal. Goals can be highly specific or more general. You might have one big goal or lots of smaller goals. The wonderful thing about climbing is that it has something for everyone. However, each individual goal will have many different paths to it, and finding the most efficient path can be a real challenge.

Your goals can be anything, but it's important to make them realistic and achievable because otherwise they're just dreams. If you currently climb Font 7a and have decided you want to climb 8b in a year but you have a full-time job and a busy family life, then it's probably not going to happen ... or you might end up in big trouble at home!

We have to think about how training for our goals can fit into or around the rest of our lives. What – if anything – are we prepared to sacrifice for our goals? How important to us are our goals?

We need to be prepared to assess our strengths and weaknesses *relative to our goals*. This will give us an idea of what we should spend time working on to reach our goals. Focusing our training specifically on

what we want to achieve is very important, otherwise we may well be wasting our time. Having goals is important for progression as it provides the motivation to work hard as well as being a good reference point for figuring out what we need to improve to achieve our goals.

Personally, I have always wanted to become a well-rounded boulderer. That's my ultimate goal. I want to be able to travel to climbing areas all over the world and stand a good chance of being able to do the best boulder problems there.

I set myself many small goals. I have a goal for every training session and every climbing trip. I even have projects on my home board that have been goals for years. But my overarching main goal has always been the same, and I constantly spend time assessing my ability with the aim of improving my weaknesses so that I can become well-rounded and skilled across the whole range of climbing styles.

The problem-solving aspect of climbing is the thing I enjoy the most. I have never fancied spending months on end trying exactly the same moves over and over and over. I can see the appeal of this style of climbing, but for me it's just not as much fun as rocking up at a boulder problem and trying to climb it, right there and then. I think that's why I enjoyed my time competing – it's the ultimate test of overall climbing ability. Competition climbing showcases the strengths of the climbers but it also exposes their weakness. I liked the challenge of having to perform in any given style on demand. I guess my approach to rock climbing is similar.

What is 'training'?

Before we get stuck in, we should consider what training is by its traditional definition: **Purposefully subjecting the body to physical or mental stress in order to promote adaptations which make it better at dealing with that stress over time.**

Training requires:
Overload: In order to make strength gains, we need to train at an intensity which the body finds difficult.

Progression: Our bodies need to be constantly stimulated to make new improvements in strength. Repeating the same exercise at the same intensity over and over again will not lead to improvement.

Repetition: Our bodies will not adapt to a training stimulus instantly. We must perform an exercise over a number of sessions in order to stimulate improvement.

Recovery: Our bodies can only adapt and get stronger if we give them time to do so. Between sessions we need to rest in order for our bodies to repair and recover. Insufficient rest will mean our bodies won't be able to adapt to the training we are doing, and this will probably eventually lead to injury – or just being too knackered to climb properly.

Specificity: Our bodies will adapt to the exercises that we are doing – that's all they know! We can work as hard as we want at something, but if it's not specific to climbing, it won't improve our climbing.

And the result of stopping training is:

Reversibility: Any physical trait that has been improved by training will be reversed if the training is stopped. This doesn't happen instantly, but over time our bodies will 'de-train' and lose strength if that strength isn't being used.

CLIMBING, TRAINING & LIFE

The problem with a lot of information about training is that it's often unrealistically focused towards hypothetical individuals with unlimited time, facilities, funds and motivation. If this is you, then it will be easy to optimise how and when you train, what you eat, when you go climbing, when you see the physio and so on. But, if this really is you, then you should spend most of your time going climbing, as you'll improve and have loads of fun in the process.

In reality, we have all sorts of stuff to contend with in our lives, and this tends to be the ultimate limiting factor in preventing us from reaching our maximum climbing potential. Not that this is a bad thing. Climbing is only a tiny part of life and if all we have is the ability to climb up rocks then we'll probably not have the most fulfilling time on this planet.

My hope is that this book will provide a 'normal' person with the tools to help them get the most out of their climbing, and without them having to sacrifice too much from their everyday life.

CLIMBING IS THE BEST TRAINING FOR CLIMBING

Before we get going on the training stuff, I'll cover my back with the ultimate caveat:

Training for climbing will not guarantee that you will become a good climber!

4

Climbing is an endlessly complex sport. It's not simply a matter of holding on and pulling really hard. Climbing is not a closed sport with predetermined routines or movements that need to be mastered and then performed on cue (unless you're a speed climber, then it's exactly that!). It's an open-ended sport with an infinite number of different moves to master, and it requires strength across the entire body.

The age-old saying that 'climbing is the best training for climbing' is essentially true. The more hours we spend climbing, the more we will learn about it, the more our bodies will adapt to it and the better we will become.

However, I strongly believe that **the best** way to improve climbing ability is to go climbing a lot, **and** to supplement this with very focused training to speed up the process of improvement, while hopefully also reducing the likelihood of getting injured.

The main physical factors in climbing

In my opinion, in no particular order, these are:
Finger strength/grip: The ability to hold on. This is always the most important factor in climbing. If we can't hold on to the holds, we'll not stand a chance of doing the next move. And if the holds feel big when we grab them, we'll be capable of moving much further off them on the next move.

Footwork: The ability to weight our feet as we climb. Having our feet on is one thing, but getting as much weight through them as we possibly can is the goal.

Flexibility/mobility: The ability to get our bodies into the positions which are the most efficient for each move. I don't think there is such a thing as a climber who is too mobile.

Connection: The ability to move everything in sync, so that our bodies can flow upwards with minimal thought or superfluous movement. This is very hard to 'train' – it is generally learned through years of climbing a lot and by practising with purpose.

Core strength: The ability to get the lower body into the correct position and keep it there while we move upwards. Comes from the shoulders, stomach, lower back and glutes. But it can also involve everything from our toes to our fingertips. This is often mistaken for the ability to do a sit-up, or for having a six-pack.

Pulling strength: The ability to move between the holds. Comes largely from the arms, shoulders and back.

Pushing strength: The ability to press down on holds. Mostly comes from the legs, or occasionally the arms when in grooves, on mantelshelves or on a lot of modern competition-style boulder problems.

Of course, we also need good movement skills, steely determination and a strong mental game, but each of these would need an entire other book to do them justice.

GENETICS

Everyone is different. We come in all sorts of shapes and sizes. Genetics play a huge part in our overall outcomes. This applies to climbing, just as it does everything else in life.

There's no guarantee that you or I can become the world's best climber by training more than anyone else. At the top end of climbing, a lot of people train very hard, but very few people become the best. Everybody is dealt a particular skill set – for some people this will overlap well with climbing, but for others it might not.

Some people have very long arms, some people are naturally quite light for their height, some people have ridiculous levels of finger strength without seeming to really work at it, some people can do a one-arm pull-up off the couch. These are all useful traits for climbing, but non-climbers wouldn't necessarily see them as beneficial. The problem is that it isn't always clear where our natural abilities lie and how well our bodies suit climbing until we start getting stuck in and testing out our limits.

The challenge for us all is to make the most out of the hand we are dealt. Whether or not we have the genetic ability to be the best shouldn't affect our ability to get a huge amount of enjoyment out of climbing. The really fun part is to see how far we can go with what we have, and to try to enjoy working it out along the way. We have to figure out how to stack the deck in our favour, and make our strengths and weaknesses work for us, not against us.

As I mentioned before, I don't think I'm genetically all that gifted for climbing. While I have naturally quite long arms and wide shoulders (thanks, Mum and Dad), I am also naturally fairly heavy (for a climber) and have sweaty hands – not necessarily ideal traits for hard climbing.

Fortunately, I was gifted with and encouraged by my parents to develop a strong work ethic, a high boredom threshold and the ability to suffer and try hard. I also can't stand imperfection in anything. These mental traits have served me very well over the years – in some respects!

I grew up climbing with a friend who was physically the opposite to me. Slim, light, fit, naturally strong fingers, handsome etc. He could casually do a one-arm pull-up on a mono without any real effort. An amazing training partner. But, ultimately for him, climbing just wasn't that much of a challenge so he never got truly stuck in, and never really achieved anything near his potential. Not that that is a bad thing. He always was, and continues to be, a lovely chap and he got a lot of enjoyment out of climbing.

I think of Shauna as having some fairly good genetic traits for climbing (which isn't to say she doesn't work really hard too!). She's got long arms and naturally strong fingers, and she's mentally very tough. She also adapts to training unusually quickly. Just a few sessions doing a new exercise is enough to see her making massive improvements. Being fairly

SHAUNA COXSEY ON *PILGRIMAGE*, PARISELLA'S CAVE, WALES.
© *NED FEEHALLY*

short often holds her back on longer moves, but when she's on small holds on steep terrain, or on very bunched footholds, she's just unstoppable.

It's worth assessing where your genetic strengths and weaknesses lie. It's great for getting the excuses in, and it can also keep your ego in check when you find something easy! You can decide when it's best to work your weaknesses, or just roll with your strengths. Sometimes it's great to climb on things which suit you. And knowing exactly what you're bad at is a good thing for your training.

The great thing about climbing is it's totally random with many different avenues to explore, so there is something for everyone.

CAN ANYONE CLIMB HARD?

I think the average climber is capable of reaching a decent level with determination, good facilities and the ability to train without getting injured. But can anyone climb F9a or Font 8b and above?

No, probably not.

I suspect that a lot of people have the genetic, physical ability to do so, but don't have the mental fortitude – they can't be arsed – or the time and/or funds to do so. While others are mentally very strong but they just lack the physiological traits required for hard climbing.

The main limiting factor for the average climber is mental, not physical. A lot of people like the *idea* of being a very good climber, but aren't prepared to *work* for it, or change anything in their lives to make it happen. Generally speaking, the best climbers are the ones who are prepared to work the hardest.

If you're a physiological outlier – you're particularly tall, or particularly short, for example – you'll be able to reach a higher maximal level more quickly (if you can find specific projects that fit your body), but your progress will probably slow down more quickly as you'll run out of things that suit you and you'll have to start working on your weaknesses in order to keep improving and climbing harder.

Every genetic trait – physiological and psychological – sits on a bell curve. The majority of people sit around the middle of the curve, close to the 50th percentile. The number of people reduces as you get further away from the 50th percentile.

It's often assumed that climbing grades are absolute, and correct. They are not! They are based on subjective assessments from various ascensionists. As a climb gets more ascents the grade is more likely to settle down as a consensus on the route or problem's difficulty is reached.

So, grades are based on the average ascensionist. The further from average that you are the less grades will apply to you! I suspect it's easier for a physiological outlier to climb a small number of hard climbs than it is for an average person. However, the physiological outlier will have a much-reduced list of things that fit their body type, and most climbing might even feel harder than average for them.

On the other hand, the average person will have a much bigger pool of things that they can theoretically do, but likely fewer things that will feel particularly easy for them.

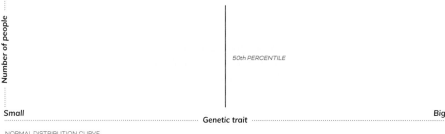

Number of people

50th PERCENTILE

Small

Genetic trait

Big

NORMAL DISTRIBUTION CURVE.

SHAUNA COXSEY TRAINING AT THE CLIMBING HUB, BRADFORD.
© *BAND OF BIRDS*

Height is the classic example here. Imagine an average climber who climbs with a tall and gangly climber. The tall climber will of course find the slabby/vertical, reachy climbs and dynos easier than the average climber. But the average climber might find any sort of bunched move, steep climb, rockover or toe hook easier than the tall climber.

But also your finger size, shoulder width, thumb size, torso length, leg length, how brave you are, how hard you are willing to try – ad infinitum – are all traits which vary from person to person and will determine how easy or difficult a particular climb will feel to you.

With the recent growth of climbing, training facilities and knowledge are becoming more and more advanced. While at the cutting edge grades are advancing slowly, the level of the average climber has shot up.

At the cutting edge of rock climbing the limiting factor now seems to be finding bits of rock which are hard enough to be a real challenge but are not impossible. While also fitting the specific morphology of the potential first ascensionist. The difficulty of a rock climb is – should be! – dictated by the randomness of nature. Millions of years of erosion doesn't necessarily cater for really good, hard rock climbs.

Perhaps the future of hard climbing is purely indoors where difficulty is theoretically infinite and can be tweaked and adjusted indefinitely, and replicated around the world for everybody to try?

Glossary of basic training terminology

Strength: The amount of force your body can exert against resistance.

Power: Strength x Speed – the ability to exert strength rapidly.

Recruitment: A measure of how many motor units are working in a muscle. The more motor units that are working, the more strength your muscles can output.

Neuromuscular: Relating to the nerves and the muscles which they control. Muscles can only switch on and provide strength when a nerve tells them to do so.

Density: Relating to the cross-sectional area of connective tissue/muscle.

Isometric: Static – an isometric exercise involves using strength but not causing movement around a joint.

Plyometric: Getting muscles to exert maximum force in the shortest time possible.

Rep: A single repetition of an exercise. For example, one pull-up, or one hang on a fingerboard.

Set: A work/rest cycle involving a number of reps with a defined rest period between each.

Load: The total amount of resistance used to perform an exercise.

Aerobic: Requiring oxygen to produce fuel.

Anaerobic: Not requiring oxygen to produce fuel.

Hold vs grip?: A hold is something that you grab on to. A grip position is the shape your fingers and hands make in order to hold on in a particular way. For example, you might use a crimp grip on a very small incut hold.

A SHORT HISTORY OF TRAINING FOR CLIMBING

With the help of Jerry Moffatt I have tried to outline the history of training for climbing over the last few decades. It's fascinating to see how far it's come in such a short time. You'll be pleased to see that both training techniques and climbing fashion have moved on a bit since the early days.

1950s AND 1960s
John Gill saw climbing, especially bouldering, as a gymnastic pursuit rather than purely a training exercise for mountain climbing. He considered bouldering to have artistic merit beyond the pure difficulty of the climbing. He introduced the use of chalk to climbers and carried the strength and training methods he learned as a gymnast into the world of climbing. He was doing one-arm front levers in the 1960s!

LATE 1970s
People mainly did pull-ups and traversed on stone buildings. Jim Collins made the first ascent of *Genesis* (5.12+) in Eldorado Canyon – the hardest route in the world at the time. He trained for it by traversing along buildings.

EARLY 1980s
John Bachar set up a training area with a 'fingerboard' in Camp 4, Yosemite. He called it 'Gunsmoke'. *Cool name, huh?* Bachar originally trained as a pole vaulter and was coached by Joe Douglas, who later became Carl Lewis's coach. This background wore off on Bachar, who seems to have been the first person to structure his fingerboard training and apply athletic training methods to climbing in general.

Jerry visited the US, climbed with Bachar and brought a lot of Bachar's ideas back to the UK with him.

At this point, bouldering was only ever really done as training for routes.

JERRY MOFFATT AND BEN MOON TRAINING HARD BACK IN THE
EARLY 1990S. © *JERRY MOFFATT*

LATE 1980s

Wolfgang Güllich and Norbert Sandner
invented the first campus board in Nuremberg,
and a few people started to build their own.
Jerry visited and started to add a few other
holds to the campus board so that he could
make up problems rather than just laddering
up the rungs.

Home walls started to be built in the cellars of
Sheffield. At first these were horizontal roofs
which people campussed across. The idea
was that if you could climb without your feet,
things would feel easy once you went outside
and had your feet on the rock! But it was soon
realised that climbing with your feet on would
be a bit more useful ...

JERRY MOFFATT ON THE CAMPUS BOARD. © *JERRY MOFFATT*

Jerry built a 45-degree board in his cellar, 'just about the best training device' he ever used. He made the holds out of wood as resin holds were hard to obtain at the time. He wanted to train on poor footholds, so he made these himself by driving a screw into the board and smearing resin over the screw head to make a small lump to stand on.

Jerry made himself a fingerboard in 1987 which he used to train on and test his strength when he travelled. It had a 10-millimetre edge, a 20-millimetre edge and a few finger pockets. He used to do pull-ups and one-armed hangs on it. It's still screwed on to the back of the original campus board in Nuremberg.

EARLY 1990s

Commercial climbing walls started to get built around the world. Resin holds became more readily available, and suddenly climbing walls could set and change boulder problems and routes.

Resin fingerboards became available.

Climbers started to get strong enough to climb on really steep terrain, rather than old-school vertical terrain.

Malcolm Smith built a home board and trained on it. In the space of a couple of years, he went from climbing F7c+ routes to repeating *Hubble* (F9a) at Raven Tor when it was one of the hardest routes in the world.

Wolfgang Güllich made the first ascent of *Action Directe* (F9a) in the Frankenjura after a lot of dedicated campus board training on one and two fingers.

LATE 1990s/EARLY 2000s

Commercial climbing walls continued to improve and became much more common, introducing a lot more people to climbing. Until now, climbing had been mostly dominated by adults, but suddenly youngsters appeared on the scene. Chris Sharma was the first of these child prodigies. In 2001 he climbed *Realization (Biographie)* in Céüse, the world's first F9a+.

Bouldering became accepted as a sport in its own right, and in 2000 Fred Nicole climbed *Dreamtime* in Cresciano, the world's first Font 8c.

Down-turned climbing shoes appeared, helping climbers on really steep terrain.

LATE 2000s
Modern mega climbing walls started to open. Beastmaker started to produce fingerboards. While training had been going on in the background for years, it suddenly became widely accepted and adopted by many climbers. Fingerboard training was no longer solely the preserve of climbing geeks. Everyone was getting involved!

Climbing styles changed. Climbers started to develop more feature-based climbing, rather than sticking to overhanging crimp climbing.

Climbing shoe technology developed, allowing for more difficult heel hooks and toe hooks, and opening up more opportunities for climbers.

EARLY 2010s
Eva López started to publish scientific papers on finger strength training – probably the first time that climbing training had been scientifically researched. The internet became a valuable resource for training information, albeit a busy one!

Training boards started to become more popular, appearing in most large climbing walls.

Climbers started to develop a much more dynamic style, rather than the old-school 'lock off on a hold as hard as you can' style.

LATE 2010s
The rise of the freaks! The large number of people being introduced to climbing led to many freakishly strong climbers appearing. Feats of strength that were rare 10 years ago became commonplace.

When we first made the Beastmaker 2000, very few people could one-arm hang on the bottom middle edge. People could now hang off it with 20 kilograms added! Over the decade, the average strength of climbers went through the roof. Also, as climbers began to start climbing much younger, they now had the time to develop amazing technical ability to go with their strength.

EARLY 2020s AND ONWARDS …
Where will the future take us? The difficulty of rock climbs is dictated randomly by nature. As rock climbing levels advance, the chances of finding a rock that's hard enough while not being impossible gets smaller and smaller.

As I write this, climbing is set to make its (delayed) debut appearance at the Olympics. Love it or loathe it, this is a very significant step for climbing to take and it will introduce the sport to many more people across the globe.

TRAINING
STRUCTURE

STRUCTURING YOUR TRAINING

Climbing is a complex sport. It's not just a physical pursuit. It's tactical and technical. It can rely heavily on the seasons and the weather, and it has an enormous psychological component. All of these factors make training for climbing surprisingly difficult and very non-linear.

I think that for the average climber, too much structure when it comes to training is not a good thing. I know this sounds like a cop-out, as you probably want to read about what to do and when to do it, but climbing is so difficult to quantify, and trying to fit it in around an ordinary life means that whatever you do to train for it, it won't be optimal.

Training in a slightly suboptimal way, but being persistent, is likely to yield better long-term results than executing a single perfectly orchestrated training cycle and then losing interest and not really training again. The climbers who continue to improve and who make the most overall progress are the ones who are the most consistent with their training over the years.

The best thing you can do is keep turning up and keep trying hard – without overdoing it and without injuring yourself. Who knows, you might even enjoy it too!

When I'm training hard, I'll have a number of sessions that I want to fit in each week, but beyond that I'll have no plan. I will want to do a few different fingerboard sessions and a couple of board sessions. I also like to fit in a more general climbing session, either indoors or out.

I like to be able to adjust my training to fit around everything else that's going on in my life, and also adjust each session according to how I'm feeling on the day. Some days it just doesn't work, and I have to be able to take a step back and stop or change to something else. Shauna tells me this is something that I have to be regularly reminded about ...

On other days I might feel much better than expected so I can have a harder session than I anticipated. Learning how to gauge this is very important. But it will be very personal to you, and not necessarily that easy to figure out.

Of course, this rather anarchic approach to training may not be scientifically the best way of getting the absolute most out of your body, but if you're reading this book you probably have a job and climb for fun. There's a certain percentage of performance that 'normal' people are quite happy to sacrifice. Even the keenest climbers don't realistically do absolutely everything they can to improve their climbing (think, beer). And if you're the sort of person that already does, then you don't need to read this book!

© ALEX MEGOS

I think finger strength training should be maintained year-round to some degree. Of course, it's beneficial to alter the stimulus on the body by mixing up the specific methods, but finger strength takes so long to develop that it should be seen as a training constant.

The same goes for flexibility and mobility. If you can keep on top of it year-round, your body will be a lot happier in general, and probably much less injury prone.

All other elements of training can come and go depending on your focus, but having strong, healthy fingers and good flexibility will set you up to climb well.

Shauna has had to train much more carefully over the years – competitions throw all sorts at you, especially the combined format at the Olympics. She tends to have a much more detailed plan, simply because she has a lot more to fit in and get better at. However, there's still a lot of flexibility built into her training plan. If she's not feeling it, she will either stop for the day or change to training something else. Ultimately, if she's enjoying what she's doing, she puts a lot more effort into it and gets much better results from it.

JOHN COEFIELD ON *JUST TOE IT*, BRIONE, SWITZERLAND.
© *DAVE PARRY*

Before planning your training, consider the following:

/ Your goal(s).
/ What you need/want to train to achieve your goals.
/ How much time you have available for training.
/ How much you are willing to sacrifice in order to achieve your goals.

When planning your training, consider the following:

/ Always prioritise fingers and flexibility. Unless of course you don't need to work on those things at all, which is unlikely.
/ Always do high-intensity strength training (fingerboarding, hard bouldering, board climbing, and so on) when you're fresh and well rested. Keep the quality high.

/ Respond to how you're feeling and adjust your sessions accordingly.
/ Have periods when you concentrate on training and periods when you concentrate on performing.
/ Climbing is highly technical and complex. You need to really concentrate on what you're doing, and this gets harder the more tired you get.
/ You can get away with doing some lower-intensity endurance training, mileage or general conditioning when you're a little fatigued.

Keep turning up. Keep trying hard. Keep enjoying it. The rest will follow.

TAPERING

Tapering is the practice of reducing the training load on your body to allow it to recover and regroup, while remaining well-honed for the task at hand. You don't want to train really hard for a trip, climb or competition and feel tip-top, only to arrive and realise that you're exhausted from training so hard that can't climb your best. Usually when a trip or objective is looming you feel the pressure to up your training, a bit like cramming the night before an exam.

Generally, reducing training volume while maintaining a high intensity is the best method for tapering. The body will get the correct stimulus to keep things firing but it will not get worn out by hours and hours of repetitive load.

Before a trip I tend to have a couple of weeks of tapering off. I want to feel good, so I keep climbing on hard problems and doing maximal fingerboard sessions, but I reduce my training time down to about 40 per cent of normal over the course of those two weeks. It can make me feel lazy, but I know I will also feel great when I finally arrive at my destination, fresh and strong. Tapering also lets my skin recover from all that training. Arriving on a trip with battered skin is a mug's game!

Summary

Consider your goals before you start to train.

Always prioritise finger strength training.

Always do high-intensity strength training when you are most rested.

Be prepared to adapt a session to suit exactly how you're feeling on the day.

Don't expect to train at 100 per cent and then go and climb at your best the next day: rest and recovery are important.

Try to separate periods of hard training from periods of performance for the best results.

UPPER BODY, HAND & FINGER ANATOMY

To help us to visualise exactly what's going on when we climb or train, it's worth taking a look inside the human body. Everyone knows we have biceps (whether they're big or small), but who knows about the pronator teres or the interossei, for example? These muscles are crucial for climbing, but they don't often pop up in conversations, so you might not have heard of them.

While it's not essential to know exactly how the body is operating, I find it very useful to be able to picture which muscles are working and when. This is in part because it helps me to make sure I am training correctly, and also because it really helps me to understand why

things hurt and what I can do to stop them from hurting.

This might all seem complicated, but the musculoskeletal system is simply a set of levers and pulleys that are operated by pulling on some strings. The body is essentially a simple machine, despite its unquestionable complexity.

Of course, it's not possible to cover absolutely everything here, nor with absolute accuracy, but the following illustrations should give a simple yet pretty solid introduction to the most important muscles that we use when we go climbing.

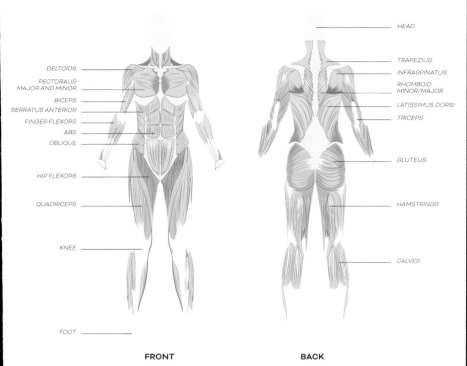

DELTOIDS
PECTORALIS MAJOR AND MINOR
BICEPS
SERRATUS ANTERIOR
FINGER FLEXORS
ABS
OBLIQUE
HIP FLEXORS
QUADRICEPS
KNEE
FOOT

HEAD
TRAPEZIUS
INFRASPINATUS
RHOMBOID MINOR/MAJOR
LATISSIMUS DORSI
TRICEPS
GLUTEUS
HAMSTRINGS
CALVES

FRONT

BACK

BODY OVERVIEW

I guess it's all fairly obvious. Climbers tend to have pretty well-developed upper body muscles due to the demands placed on the body by climbing. Big lats, big shoulders and big pecs are all hallmarks of the climber's body.

The shoulder is the body's most mobile joint, which is great for climbing, but it does mean it's inherently quite unstable as a result. The core muscles all have to work hard when we climb to (hopefully) keep our arms and legs working together as a unit – or perhaps they just help swing our legs around when we're campussing through the crux sequence?

However, we should not treat our legs as an afterthought! Much of our weight will generally be going through the legs, even on steep terrain. If we have to carry our legs around with us then we may as well make the most of them when we climb. The quadriceps work really hard on rockovers and dynamic moves, and the hamstrings and glutes are essential for heel hooks and clawing in on steep terrain.

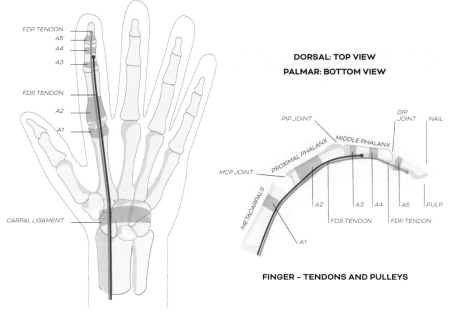

DORSAL: TOP VIEW

PALMAR: BOTTOM VIEW

FINGER – PALMAR VIEW (LEFT HAND)

FINGER – TENDONS AND PULLEYS

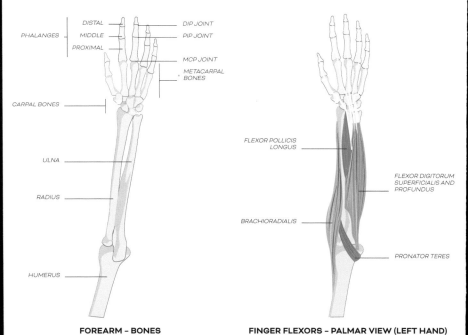

FOREARM – BONES

FINGER FLEXORS – PALMAR VIEW (LEFT HAND)

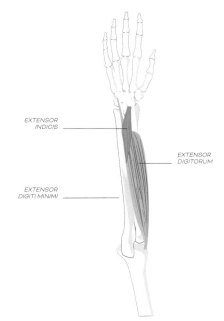

FINGER EXTENSORS – DORSAL VIEW (LEFT HAND)

EXTENSOR INDICIS

EXTENSOR DIGITORUM

EXTENSOR DIGITI MINIMI

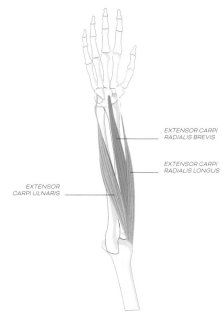

WRIST EXTENSORS – DORSAL VIEW (LEFT HAND)

EXTENSOR CARPI RADIALIS BREVIS

EXTENSOR CARPI RADIALIS LONGUS

EXTENSOR CARPI ULNARIS

ARMS AND FINGERS: TEAMWORK

In each of our fingers we have two flexor tendons which curl our fingers into a gripping position and allow us to hold on. The FDP (flexor digitorum profundus) flexes the tip of the finger, while the FDS (flexor digitorum superficialis) flexes the middle joint of the finger. These flexor tendons are attached to our finger flexor muscles which pull on the tendons to allow us to hold on.

The tendons run through the pulleys in the wrist, hand and fingers (A1 to A5) which keep the tendons close to the bones allowing our fingers to work properly.

On the opposite side of our forearms we have the finger and wrist extensor muscles. These straighten our fingers (bend our wrists upwards), or work to stabilise the joints while we grab on with our finger flexors.

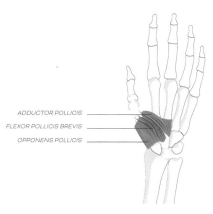

ADDUCTOR POLLICIS
FLEXOR POLLICIS BREVIS
OPPONENS POLLICIS

THUMB FLEXORS – PALMAR VIEW

In addition to the flexors in our fingers, the flexor muscles in our thumbs are crucial when we are pinching as they produce opposition against the fingers.

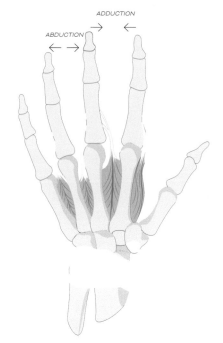

HAND ANATOMY – INTEROSSEI (DORSAL VIEW, LEFT HAND)

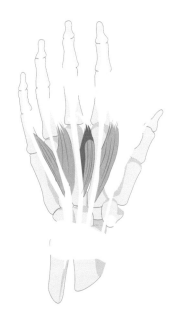

HAND ANATOMY – LUMBRICALS (DORSAL VIEW, LEFT HAND)

HAND

I think the anatomy of our hands is especially important. A lot of people don't even know that their hands have small muscles in them! These muscles are crucial for climbing, but they are not well understood. Occasionally, pulley injuries are in fact misdiagnosed problems with the muscles in the hand – it's always worth bearing this in mind if you feel pain in a finger.

The interossei are tiny little muscles which adduct and abduct the fingers (move them from side to side) and they play an important role in stabilising our fingers as we hold on, especially when we grab a crimp or an uneven hold which splays the fingers at unusual angles. They arise from your metacarpal bones (the bones in our palm) and attach to

the bones of the proximal phalanges (the first finger bone, closest to the palm).

The lumbricals are another small set of muscles within the palm of the hand. They arise from the flexor tendons (unusual, as most muscles originate from a bone) and attach to the proximal phalanges (first finger bone) via the extensor expansion – so they actually attach to the top of the fingers. Lumbricals help to flex the metacarpophalangeal (MCP) joint (first knuckle) which contributes to our finger strength. They work the hardest when we are holding on with straight fingers (imagine a big wide pinch, or grabbing a volume) as in this position our flexor tendons can't work effectively because our fingers are not flexed.

FINGER STRENGTH

© MARTIN SMITH

WHAT IS 'FINGER STRENGTH'?

Climbers use this term to describe our ability to hang on to some handholds. Better finger strength allows us to hold on to smaller or poorer handholds. As a climber, this is useful, as generally the handholds become worse as the difficulty of the climbing increases. So, the more 'finger strength' we have, the more likely we are to be able to hold on and move between the handholds.

Finger strength is usually the limiting factor for climbers who would like to improve. All of the best climbers in the world have very strong fingers. We can get away with weaknesses in other areas, but if we can't hold on to the wall then we can't climb. Simple.

WHERE DOES FINGER STRENGTH COME FROM?

Finger strength is the combination of many structures in the hand and forearm working together.

It's not immediately obvious where our finger or grip strength comes from. We don't have muscles in our fingers. They're just bony and thin. So how do we hold on to handholds?

Generally speaking, climbing-specific grip strength comes from the finger flexor muscles (the bottom of the forearm if the palm is placed flat on a table (page 24)) in our fore-arms contracting and curling our fingers on to the handholds. As we grip the holds, our finger flexors hold the fingers isometrically (statically) around the handhold, keeping the rest of us attached (hopefully) to the holds. Which means we can climb between them.

But there's more to the story. Our finger flexors tighten the flexor tendons. These run through a number of pulleys in our fingers (page 24). Pulleys are ligaments which hold the tendons on to the bones of the finger, and act literally as pulleys to transfer the force of a contracting forearm muscle into usable grip strength in the fingers. Pulleys allow us to move our fingers with huge amounts of dexterity and accuracy, and also close them around handholds with a lot of strength. Without pulleys, if we tried to hold on to a handhold, our tendons would pull away from the bones in our hands. Climbing would be impossible!

The commonly used analogy for pulleys and tendons is to imagine the eyelets through which fishing line passes along a fishing rod. Under tension, the fishing line bends the rod, but the eyelets hold the line close to the rod as it bends.

So, when we climb, our finger flexor muscles contract, pulling the fingers into a gripping position. Under load, the tendons and pulleys have a frictional interaction, which adds to the isometric strength in our fingers, making them more difficult to uncurl than the strength in our flexor muscles alone would suggest.

Therefore, training our 'finger strength' will increase the force that our forearm muscles can apply, but it will also increase tendon and pulley thickness/density, increasing the propensity for frictional interactions, which adds to our ability to hold on to handholds.

Our finger strength is also dependent on additional factors:

/   Our hands contain many small muscles, including lumbricals and interossei, as well as all the thumb muscles. All of these are essential for climbing-specific grip strength.
/   The wrists have muscles associated with moving and holding them in place as we climb – the flexor and extensor carpi radialis muscles, for instance.
/   And, finally, the finger extensor group of forearm muscles (the top of the forearm if the palm is placed flat on a table) which act with the finger flexor muscles to stabilise our hands and fingers as we climb.

THE AUTHOR ON *SATAN I HELVETE*, COQUIBUS LONGS VAUX, FONTAINEBLEAU, FRANCE. © *LEO MOGER*

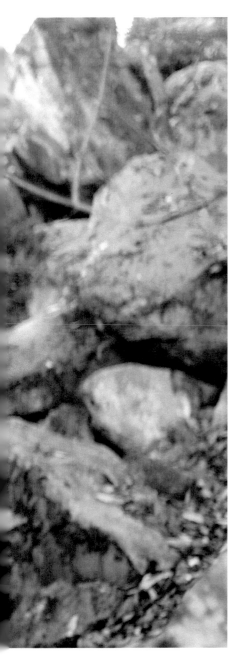

FINGER MORPHOLOGY

As well as finger strength, the exact size, shape and build of our hands will affect how well we can hold on.

Everyone's fingers are different. Different lengths, different thicknesses, different fingernails, different amounts of flesh in the pads of the fingers. Each different finger type will lend itself to different things.

I have quite fat, fleshy finger pads. This is great for friction climbing and slopers as they have a fairly large surface area, but it's not so good on really small holds where the fleshy padding rolls about under load. Shauna has small, bony fingers with tough ends. They are great on really small holds and she very rarely has to full crimp anything as her fingers are absolutely solid on tiny edges even in a half crimp position. However, tiny hands aren't great on big slopers or pinches as they have limited surface area for creating friction.

Differences in the lengths of individual fingers is also interesting. Some people have a very short pinkie finger compared to their other three fingers. This often means they struggle to get the pinkie involved, especially on crimps. As a result, these people tend to be very good at crimping on their front three fingers as their pinkie can't really bring anything to the party.

Some people have a very long middle finger, meaning that it's often going to be bent to some degree, even on very open-handed holds.

To be honest, none of this really matters. We have the hands we have. It's interesting to see how different people's hands work. And it can be great to have plenty of micro excuses – 'your pinkie is shorter than mine, that's why I can't do it', and so on.

IMPROVING FINGER STRENGTH

Fortunately for climbers, the body is very good at adapting to stresses. This means that with repeated load we can increase the strength and size of the muscles, tendons and ligaments that are associated with finger strength. Be aware that increases in muscle strength occur over a matter of weeks, but notable increases in the thickness and density of tendons and ligaments occur much more slowly, over months and years.

For many people, especially those with a young 'training age', simply going climbing regularly is enough to stimulate their bodies to adapt and increase their finger strength.

Of course, just 'going climbing' is a pretty blunt tool, and if this is your only tactic then eventually you may reach a point where your finger strength seems to plateau.

At this point you may want to consider other ideas so that you can make further gains in your finger strength. These could be:

/ Climbing in a more structured way: aiming to climb with a focus on increasing finger strength. This could mean prioritising holding on to the types of holds on which you normally struggle, or climbing on steeper terrain/steep boards which put more weight through your fingers.
/ Focused fingerboard training: targeting the specific areas of your finger strength which need work.

Summary

Finger strength is the ability to hold on to a hold or set of holds.

Finger strength comes from a combination of our forearm flexor muscles, frictional interactions between the tendons and ligaments in our hands, and the small muscles in our hands.

Increasing finger strength takes longer than we'd like! It takes months and months for tendons and ligaments to adapt to the stresses of climbing and fingerboarding.

ACTIVE VS PASSIVE FINGER STRENGTH

There is a difference
between being able to
hold on and being able
to not let go.

Climbers tend to vary in their approach to how they grab holds. Even exactly the same holds on exactly the same climb can and will be grabbed and held differently by different climbers. Some climbers will hold on really hard and squeeze the life out of the holds. Others might take a more relaxed approach and 'hook' their hands on to the holds. I classify these approaches as 'active' and 'passive', and distinguish between active and passive finger strength.

Active finger strength – favouring half crimp and full crimp positions, even on typically open-handed handholds like pockets and slopers. The thumb will usually be getting involved a lot, and really squeezing the holds. An active approach effectively uses more strength to grab on to the handholds really hard.

Passive finger strength – favouring open-handed positions on most handholds, and using friction rather than strength within the hand in order to hold on.

Of course, holding on to any handhold requires strength, but the crucial difference is in how active the muscles within the hand itself are.

Climbers might favour or default to an active or passive approach to gripping because of their favoured rock types, where they initially learned to climb, or their physiology. It could even have something to do with past injuries. Rock types with more friction, or big bolt-on holds, will develop a more passive style of holding on, while learning to climb on steep surfaces, on small holds or on slicker rock, will lead to a more active gripping style.

Climbers who spend more time route climbing are likely to have a more passive gripping style. This allows them to use the minimum amount of energy to hold each position, and by using less energy to climb they will get less pumped.

Climbers who boulder more don't need to worry so much about conserving energy, and as a result they often grip harder on to the holds. This works well for short, intense sequences, but it's important to learn when it's OK to relax on the holds, and when to hold on as hard as possible.

Neither is wrong, but both styles of gripping are worth thinking about.

You can always learn how to transfer an active grip to a more passive gripping situation. **Once you have the strength for a good active grip, you can choose whether to use it or use a more passive approach.** But if you don't have the strength to use an active grip in the first place, you won't have the option of being able to use it.

DRAG.

OPEN HAND.

HALF CRIMP.

CRIMP.

FULL CRIMP.

PASSIVE (LEFT) VS ACTIVE GRIP ON A SLOPER.

TRAINING ACTIVE GRIP STRENGTH

If you feel that you need to work on your active grip strength then you should focus on half crimp, full crimp and pinch positions. Anything that really engages the muscles in your hands.

During a standard climbing session, you should concentrate on actively holding on harder to holds during moves, rather than just dangling from them. Set yourself moves between holds which are not positive – flat edges, pinches, slopers with thumb catches and so on – and think carefully about how you are holding the holds as you move between them.

Climbing on steep terrain such as boards is great for working active grips as you have to hold on really hard to control swings and move your feet about – you can't just rely on friction to keep you on the wall. And, generally, the smoother the holds the better, as you'll need to hold on even harder to stay on – wooden handholds, rather than resin, are perfect in this respect.

But ultimately it comes back to your goals. Consider the climbs you'd like to do and the things you'd like to achieve, and then think about whether you need to be able to really crush holds, or just hang from them – and then adjust your training accordingly.

Personally, I always default to a more open-handed, passive position when I'm climbing. And as I start to get tired, I tend to head in this direction. I don't find reeling in a crimp a natural thing to do. As a result, I have spent countless hours working on the more active end of my finger strength – lots of crimping

ACTIVELY GRIPPING ON THE BOARD.

It is much harder to transfer a more passive gripping style into an active gripping situation if you don't have the strength to do it. Imagine trying to open-hand a slick granite pinch on an overhang. Good luck with that.

I recommend training active grip positions when possible, but remember that being comfortable with both active and passive gripping styles is necessary for climbing well on a range of hold styles and rock types.

and climbing on small, crimpy pinches. Initially this was on the fingerboard, and then during general climbing and board sessions.

A tip I have for working on this specific type of active strength is to set yourself problems which feature narrow moves on thin, crimpy pinches. This way you can't turn the holds into sidepulls – you'll be forced to squeeze them hard when you come in close on the narrow moves. This kind of training has had a huge positive effect on my active finger strength.

Shauna has a very active gripping style. She can really crush holds and hold on very hard. She often gets her thumb involved, pinching or squeezing the handholds. I don't think I've ever seen her even open-hand a pocket, because she can usually get all of her fingers into most two-finger pockets and half crimp them!

A lot of active finger strength comes from the engagement of the muscles in the hand and/or thumb. When you open-hand a hold, your lumbricals and interossei don't tend to do too much of the work. When you crimp a small handhold as hard as possible, these muscles are all engaged to keep the hand in the most advantageous position for holding on – keeping the knuckles bent.

Taking care of and strengthening these small muscles is important for any climber, but especially for those who want to improve their active finger strength. See chapter 16.

Summary

Active gripping isn't necessarily natural, but it allows you to hold on and pull really hard! Which is almost always a good thing on hard moves.

Active gripping allows you to maintain more stability through the handholds as you move your body.

Passive gripping relies a lot more on friction and skin, and so only works well on the right kinds of handholds. But it does require less energy in order to hold on.

What can I do?

To improve your active grip strength, concentrate on really gripping the holds as you climb.

Climb on steep terrain on pinches, or holds with a very smooth texture, as this will teach you to hold on really hard.

Climb on steep boards with lots of small wooden holds – this is perfect for training active grip strength ... provided you concentrate your efforts on trying to develop your active grip strength! See chapter 10.

TACTICS PART 1

There are a few things I have learned over the years which have helped my climbing no end. Something here might be new to you and may well help your climbing too. This list makes me realise how ridiculous our sport is! Flick to pages 84 and 142 for more.

WARMING UP

Over the years I have found it very beneficial to dial in a good warm-up routine. For me, this involves a fingerboard. I find that if I have a standardised warm-up on a fingerboard then I can gauge how I'm feeling as I warm up and I can ensure that my fingers are 100 per cent ready to pull hard when I climb. I use a portable fingerboard when I'm at the crag, and a wall-mounted fingerboard when I am at the climbing wall or before training on my board.

RESTING

I've found that resting between attempts is as much about allowing my skin to cool down and dry out as letting my muscles recover. Cold, dry skin has a lot more grip on holds than warm, sweaty skin. When our skin feels cold to the touch, we'll have much more grip than when our hands feel warm to the touch. The best way of cooling the hands down seems to be to rest. I know climbers who put their hands on a rock to cool them down. I find that this doesn't help me much as my hands tend to get sweaty and damp when they're held against a surface for any length of time. Getting some breeze over my hands – from the wind, using a fan or swinging them around a bit if there is no breeze – is the best way to cool and dry my skin.

CRAG FAN

In my opinion, cold hands are essential for hard climbing. When it's practical and the weather demands it, I like to take an 18-volt battery fan out to the crag. The added wind can boost the conditions a lot. It's sometimes even worth the faff of carrying it in! On a warm day, a fan can also keep the insects away.

WIND

Too much wind can be a nightmare to climb in, but a good breeze is essential for getting perfect conditions (unless it's a warm or humid breeze, which will bring in extra moisture).

SUN

I much prefer to climb on overcast days or on shady problems. Be careful to choose a climbing venue depending on the conditions on the day. A south-facing suntrap might be a good bet on a very cold day, or it might be the worst possible choice on a hot day.

TEMPERATURE

I like cold conditions. My body works best between about 5 and 10 °C, but my skin works best at about 0 °C. Any warmer than this and I simply don't function as well. Figure out your optimal temperature range and use this to your advantage. This might mean heading out climbing earlier in the day, or waiting a bit longer for things to cool down, or wearing more or less clothing while you climb.

HUMIDITY

The lower the better. Unfortunately, living in the UK, it rarely drops below 70 per cent, and there's nothing we can really do about it.

Apart from complain and check the weather forecast to plan our sessions as well as possible! If you're climbing in a desert, then very low humidity is more likely to cause you problems. Products like Rhino Skin Solutions Spit, or simply wetting your hands before chalking up, can help you to gain some adhesion on 'glassy skin' days, when the humidity is very low, or when you're training on wooden holds or fingerboards.

SHOES

Choose shoes that work for the boulder problem or climb you are on. It's rare that I climb in only one pair of shoes on a particular day. I'll always have a few options in my bag, just in case. Different heels. Stiff. Soft. Even different rubber compounds. Different rubber types function best within certain temperature ranges. Different heel profiles will work better on different heel placements. Choose your shoes with this in mind. You can even wear different shoes on each foot.

KNEE PADS

Knee pads are great! Sometimes it's useful to duct tape them on to keep them solid, in which case you will probably want to wear shorts and shave your leg if it's hairy before taping one on to make removal afterwards a little less eye-watering! Spray adhesive can help to prevent them from moving around too, but it does get messy and is generally only used by the ultra-keen. Depending on the specific knee bar, it might be worth having a stiffer knee pad and a softer one. Some knee bars are sharp and edgy and work better with a stiff knee pad, while some are smeary and work better with a softer pad. I've even stacked two knee pads to make my leg fit a bit better in a knee bar.

INTRODUCTION TO FINGER-BOARDING

INTRODUCTION

So, we have seen where our finger strength comes from. If you want to increase your finger strength and climbing alone doesn't seem to be doing the job, the fingerboard might be for you. Bear in mind that finger strength adaptations are likely to come much more slowly than you would like. Think about fingerboard training in timescales of months and years, not days and weeks. You simply can't rush it.

Fingerboard training is, however, one of the most time-efficient ways of improving your climbing in the long run. Most climbers are ultimately going to be limited by their finger strength. Provided you have a modicum of ability, any additional finger strength gains are guaranteed to improve your climbing, whereas other types of strength training will have less of an impact. Your fingers attach you to the holds, so it makes sense to get this link of the chain as strong as you possibly can.

Fingerboarding is very simple. The idea is to hang from the fingers to encourage the body to adapt to this stress, thereby making the fingers stronger. There are many ways of training on the fingerboard, and many ways of varying the intensity of the training load.

If you are careful with how you use a fingerboard, it can be a very safe training tool. In my opinion, it is the safest way of training finger strength, when compared with climbing, board climbing and campussing, as it is very controlled, you can apply the load slowly and let go at any time.

Of course, fingerboarding has its limitations, so don't get sucked into only ever hanging off your fingers and never actually climbing, then wondering why you're still rubbish when you get back on the wall. And while I think it's the *best* way to train finger strength, it's certainly not the *only* way.

Fingerboarding is a supplementary exercise for climbing, not a replacement.

PRACTICALITIES

You need a good fingerboard. Most climbing walls will have at least one, but if you have the motivation and time then you'll be better off with one at home. Mount it in a useful place, ideally somewhere comfy and warm, perhaps close to music or a TV, so you're more likely to want to use it. The number of people who buy a fingerboard and never even put it up, or put it up and use it only once, is amazing. An unused fingerboard hanging forlornly on a wall is a sorry sight.

A good idea if you have the space is to make a training area, with your fingerboard, weights, pulleys, resistance bands etc. all in one place. The less you have to do/get out/ prepare in order to train, and the less you have to tidy up afterwards, the more likely you will be to train in the first place.

It's also worth buying a fingerboard that doesn't look horrendous, so you are more inclined to mount it in a nice place in your home or place of work. Buy a Beastmaker – I've heard they are the best.

© GIORGOS KRIKELIS

© BEN MORTON

© TAKATO IIZUKA

© MATTHEW DAVIES

© SPIKE FULLWOOD

© OLAVI SAASTAMOINEN

WHEN SHOULD I START FINGERBOARDING?

People often think you need to be climbing a certain grade, or have a certain number of years of climbing experience, before you can begin to train on a fingerboard. I don't think this is the case.

There is no reason why a relatively new climber can't do some gentle fingerboard training. Ideally you would have a few years of climbing under your belt first, but this is mainly because there is so much to learn in climbing, and as a relative beginner – having climbed for only a year or two – you'll improve so much by just going climbing. Any gains from the fingerboard will pale in comparison with simply learning how to move on the wall or rock. And going climbing is generally a lot more fun than just hanging off the fingerboard.

Once you have been climbing for a few years, then finger strength is likely to start becoming a limiting factor for you, and any gains you make will be easily transferred to your climbing as your other attributes are (hopefully) already well honed.

Climbers with many years of experience will definitely benefit from some fingerboard training, and they should already have pretty robust tendons and ligaments which can cope well with the stresses of fingerboard training, making it fairly safe.

WHAT'S THE BEST WAY OF FINGERBOARDING?

Anyone who tells you that their way is the 'best' way to fingerboard is wrong. If there was a best way, then by now we would have figured it out and we'd all be doing it! There are loads of different approaches and training methods that have been used over the years; some are probably more effective than others, but everybody is different and we need to find the approach that suits us the best. As you will see on the following pages, there are lots of methods and variables. Ultimately, the best method for you is the one which you will do and keep doing over a long period of time.

We will look at specific exercises in chapter 7, but before we do, there's some important background stuff to look at first.

FINGERBOARDING VARIABLES

HOLD TYPE
If you have a Beastmaker, then we have got you covered. You have a selection of nice edges and pockets to hang from.

If not, you want to be hanging from holds or edges which are comfy and not too sharp or rough. Try to avoid holds which sit between two joints of the finger as these can ruffle up your skin and can be quite painful to hang from.

DIFFICULTY
What's the best way to control the intensity of a fingerboard exercise?

When you're training finger strength, you need to carefully control the intensity of each hang. If it's too hard or too easy, your body won't be receiving the correct information to persuade it to get stronger.

You should aim to hang for a given time (see chapter 7), and adjust the intensity accordingly. This could be by changing the hold size, or by adjusting the load by adding or removing weight in order to get the intensity just right.

HOLD SIZE VS ADDED WEIGHT VS ONE ARM?
Of course, with fingerboarding, you can always hang on for longer, but as the main goal of fingerboard training is to increase *strength*, the longer you can hang on for, the less outright strength you are likely to develop. So, the question then is: *to increase the difficulty/intensity, is it better to hang from smaller holds, or to hang from bigger holds but add some weight?*

Both methods have their advantages and their drawbacks. Neither is the 'right' way. Once the holds become too small, friction, sweat and skin become the limiting factors rather than strength. This varies from person to person, depending on finger morphology.

TRAIN ON ONE ARM IF YOU HAVE THE STRENGTH AND STABILITY IN YOUR SHOULDER AND ARM.

Reducing hold size is great, until skin and friction (and pain!) start to limit you, but this doesn't tend to happen until you get down to holds that are smaller than about 15 millimetres in depth. At this point, you may be better off hanging from a larger hold with added weight.

Adding weight is a great way of increasing the load, but after a certain point it becomes impractical and uncomfortable as you will have all sorts of weights/anvils/tonnes of feathers dangling awkwardly from your body.

Training on one arm is a good way of ensuring you can train on bigger holds while still putting a large load through your fingers and forearm. However, as your shoulder and arm stability begin to tire, you will start to fail even though your fingers aren't necessarily fully worked. Unless you can easily do an unassisted lock-off on one arm on a jug, training finger strength on one arm might not be for you as your shoulder strength will be the limiting factor, not your finger strength. Hanging on one arm also puts a lot of stress on the skin of that hand. Of course, this depends on the total amount of weight you're hanging from your fingers, but with such a small surface area in contact with the hold or edge, skin can stop play.

GRIP TYPE

You can hang open handed, or full crimped, or in a position in between. And you can do this with all four fingers and both hands, or drop a finger (next bit, below) or an arm

(previous bit, above). Remember that when training a specific grip, it's only effective within +/- 15 degrees of that joint angle – more or less than this and you're no longer training that grip type and you might as well step off. For more on crimping see chapter 8.

REMOVING A FINGER

As a standard, you should fingerboard with all four fingers. Most handholds which you'll come across in climbing will fit four fingers, so it makes sense to train with all four fingers more than anything else. However, as you progress and gain strength, it can be useful to start training with fewer fingers. It's a good way of increasing the difficulty of a deadhang without having to keep adding more and more weight. Often when hanging on two arms, the amount of weight that needs to be added can become quite cumbersome or uncomfortable (adding 50 kilograms to a harness isn't particularly kind on the hips), so by reducing the number of fingers to three per hand, it's possible to train maximally with less added weight.

Front-three and back-three hangs are a great way of increasing the difficulty/intensity of an exercise without adding any additional weight or needing to use smaller holds or edges. Be aware that hanging with fewer than four fingers can take some getting used to as it puts uneven load across your hands, which is especially taxing on the lumbricals. Take care! And build up very slowly, rather than just piling the weight on and going for it.

INCREASE THE INTENSITY WITH THREE-FINGER HANGS.

PICKING UP A WEIGHT WITH AN EDGE IS SAFE AND MEASURABLE WITH FEWER FINGERS.

BLUETOOTH FORCE METERS SUCH AS TINDEQ CAN ALSO BE USED WITH FEWER FINGERS.

Often, the overlooked variable here is the **form** of the fingers during the deadhang. Check out the *Finger Form* section on page 66 for more information about this. Remember that you can hang on any number of fingers in an open-handed position, or a crimped position. Both are very different! Focus on exactly what you are trying to train, and adjust your form accordingly.

EVEN FEWER FINGERS

After front three and back three, we have the front two, middle two and back two groups of fingers. These can be held in an open position, or a crimped position, usually when climbing on pockets.

Pockets aren't common in all climbing areas, but they are a hold type that it's good to be familiar with. Generally, pockets are held open handed. If two-finger pockets are too easy for you, or you have a specific climb in mind that features small pockets, you can progress on to training on one-finger pockets, or monos as they're known.

FEWER FINGERS: CRIMPING!
If you have done a lot of fingerboarding in the past and would like to eek out a few more per cent from your crimp strength, then it can be very useful to train the fingers in smaller groups.

The safest and most measurable way of doing this is to pick something up using an appropriate handhold. Trying to hold your body weight on one- or two-finger crimps on a fingerboard or edge isn't a great idea – you'll probably have to take off so much weight using a pulley set-up that it's ultimately impractical. Get yourself a hold such as 15- or 20-millimetre-deep edge – I have a simple first joint hold, on a backing plate (see photo, opposite) – and attach weights to it and then pick it up. This has a few advantages: you can easily adjust the weight, you can keep a good eye on your fingers' form, and you can easily drop the weight if anything feels weird, tweaky or sore.

You can also get Bluetooth force meters which allow you do this sort of training without any weights. I use a Tindeq, which you can attach to anything. The interface is really simple and it allows you to keep an eye on the load going through your fingers in real time.

Initially, your fingers will not be used to working in smaller groups. They tend to perform as a team of four. So, take it really easy to begin with. The lumbricals and interossei will need to get used to stabilising the fingers in these positions.

This is a very intense method of training the fingers. I'd only recommend it to someone who has been climbing and training for many years.

In general ...

Start with: reducing the hold size as you improve.

Move on to: alternating between adding weight on larger holds and using smaller holds.

Once you've been doing it for a while: train on one arm (with or without added weight) or two arms with added weight. And train with fewer fingers.

However, you can vary your fingerboard sessions whatever your level. Variety is the spice of life – keep things mixed up to ensure your body doesn't get lazy. Varied training stimuli will encourage adaptations.

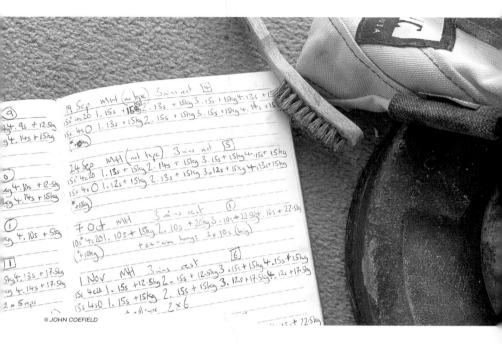

© JOHN COEFIELD

FINGERBOARDING PROGRESS

BE REALISTIC

Progress on the fingerboard absolutely is not linear. (This actually applies to all training, and even climbing in general!) You'll have good days and bad days, and good periods and bad periods. For no obvious reason you'll occasionally have a stormer and get a load of personal bests, whereas on other days you'll feel like a sack of spuds and fail on all your hangs or exercises. You need to keep your eye on the bigger picture and not focus on the current session's results. Remember that straight-up finger strength is only one part of the climbing machine.

Time of day, when you last ate, if you had a coffee, if you're stressed about something, if you slept badly, if it's warm, if the humidity is high, if you weigh more or less than normal, and so on – these can all affect your session. However, with diligent and committed training, over the course of months you should see steady progress in your finger strength.

It can be useful to record the results of your sessions. I take notes every session: I like the process of recording the data, and I find it useful to look back through it from time to time. I appreciate this isn't for everyone, but as a minimum, something as simple as recording each time you achieve a personal best at a given exercise – very infrequently these days for me! – can be very useful so that you can look back at your progress over the months and years and see which training methods seem to work best for you.

Time

Time

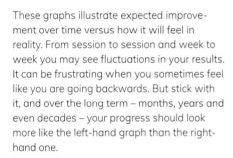

EXPECTED IMPROVEMENT OVER TIME (LEFT) VS REALITY!

These graphs illustrate expected improve-ment over time versus how it will feel in reality. From session to session and week to week you may see fluctuations in your results. It can be frustrating when you sometimes feel like you are going backwards. But stick with it, and over the long term – months, years and even decades – your progress should look more like the left-hand graph than the right-hand one.

Initially, as you start to put some time into fingerboard training, you'll notice fast improvements. This is because you make rapid neuromuscular gains when you start out – your muscles 'learn' how to work more efficiently. But, over time, your muscles will get to the point where they are working as efficiently as they can for their size. After this, the improvements come from developing muscle strength, which essentially comes down to building up more – or bigger – muscle fibres in the forearms. More muscle equals increased strength. And don't worry about your new, massive forearms weighing you down. Even in a well-developed climber, the forearms only equate to a very small percentage of total body weight.

Gains in muscle size and strength occur more slowly (over months) than neuromuscular gains (over weeks), however the gains in muscle size and strength are longer lasting.

BOREDOM THRESHOLD!

It is important to focus on finger strength as a long-term project. Climbers often get into the habit of beasting themselves for a few weeks, seeing improvements and then stopping as the rate of improvement begins to slow down. Then six months later they think, 'I need to get stronger fingers', and go back to overdoing the fingerboarding again for only a short period of time.

Fingers tend to respond really well to regular loading. Of course, totally battering yourself on the fingerboard day after day is not a good idea, nor is going from zero to hero and suddenly fingerboarding eight days a week. However, slowly building up to regularly doing short but intense fingerboard sessions is likely to not only help your fingers to get stronger, but also keep them feeling healthy and happy when you climb. A friend of mine who is a physiotherapist and a very good climber, loves to say, 'tendons don't like surprises', which sort of sums up this approach.

Treat fingerboarding as a permanent fixture in your training diary. One fingerboard session each week for one year will do you a lot more lasting good than three fingerboard sessions a week for 12 weeks followed by no fingerboarding for the rest of the year.

© ALEX MEGOS

Also, aside from muscle strength, the connective tissues and bones in the hand take time to develop and adapt to the training stimulus. The limited blood flow to the connective tissues means it takes time to get nutrients down there, and so recovery happens more slowly and gains are harder to come by – on the scale of months and years.

If you have any doubt about the way your fingers feel you should always err on the side of caution and back off. **Getting injured is exactly the opposite of training, so should be avoided at all costs!**

HUMIDITY/CHALK

Depending on where your fingerboard is mounted, you'll have to deal with fluctuating temperatures and humidity. The same fingerboard used in different environments can feel totally different. If you travel and use different fingerboards you should bear this in mind. Equally, if you see your maximum hangs get worse in the summer it is probably because you are sweating more on the holds. If you can identify these variables and consider them when you train you are more likely to be able to motivate yourself when things feel hard, rather than just

If you're struggling because your hands are too dry, then apply a little moisture or use something like Rhino Skin Solutions Spit to help you stick to the holds (see pages 69–70 for more about skin).

CORE/STABILITY ON THE FINGERBOARD

It is often overlooked, but hanging from a set of holds or edges does require body strength in order to keep you still as you hang. If you're swinging around when you're trying to hang from some small holds it will feel much harder than if you're totally still.

The less positive the holds that you're training on, the more stable you'll have to keep your body to avoid slipping off them. It can take a few hangs or even a few sessions to become familiar with where your body needs to be hanging so that you don't just swing off.

It is important to learn the starting position for each hang. This is especially true if you are new to fingerboarding and unfamiliar with it, or if you have a large pendulous weight dangling from your waist. You need to maintain tension through your shoulders and back to provide a rigid platform that is stable on the holds. And you need to lift off from a central position that creates no momentum or swing once you're hanging. See more about *Finger Form* on page 66.

stopping as you don't feel as good as you have in the past. If you're very keen, like me, it might be worth mounting a thermometer and humidity meter next to your fingerboard so you can keep an eye on conditions and cross-reference them with your results from the session. As you can tell, I enjoy the geeky approach to training!

If you're struggling because of sweaty fingers, then invest in a fan. Aim it at yourself and the fingerboard to keep you cool while you train. Remember to chalk up between every hang, and regularly brush the holds.

ADDITIONAL FINGERBOARD
EQUIPMENT
Here are a few things you might find useful
for a good fingerboard session:

Fan: keeps the air moving to prevent too
much sweat building up on your fingers and
the fingerboard.

Clock/stopwatch/timer app: keeps track of
training and rest time. Set this up in a good
spot so you can easily see it as you hang.
Having to strain to look at the timer will
literally be a pain in the neck.

Weights and pulley system: a nice, comfy
harness or dipping belt is the simplest way
of adding weight and it's easily removable
between sets. A pulley attached to a harness
is a good way of taking weight off: run a bit
of rope from your harness up through a pulley
and down to some weights; when you pull on,
you will have reduced your body weight by
whatever weight is hanging on the pulley.

Brush: keep a decent brush to hand (natural
bristles clean much better than nylon) and
keep your board clean. Brushing between
sets is a good idea and kills a bit of rest time.

Sandpaper: keeps the skin in good condition
during the session. See page 143.

Humidity meter and thermometer: good
for keeping track of conditions and useful as
these variables can have a large effect on
your exercises.

Scales: it can be worth keeping an eye on
your weight. This fluctuates so it's good to
know whether a particularly good or bad
session is because your weight is up or down
a little.

Summary

Fingerboarding is great for focused finger
strength training. It's very time efficient.

Finger strength training should be seen as
a long-term project. Gains will take months
and months to consolidate.

There is no shortcut to getting stronger
fingers. Sorry!

Only train on comfy holds.

Be very careful not to overdo it on the
fingerboard. Stop if you feel any pain or
discomfort. Finger injuries are rubbish.

What can I do?

Buy a fingerboard!

Mount it somewhere warm, dry and comfy,
with everything you need for training close
at hand.

Use it regularly.

TRACK THE CONDITIONS OF YOUR SESSIONS WITH A HUMIDITY METER.

FINGERS: GRIP TYPES & FORM

THREE-FINGER DRAG.

GRIP TYPES

THREE-FINGER DRAG (PASSIVE)

The three-finger drag relies on flexion at the DIP joint (plus a bit of bend at the PIP joint of the middle finger) and a lot of friction between the pads of the fingers and the hold.

This grip type can be very useful as it gives maximum reach, and it's possible to manoeuvre around the hold fairly well while maintaining grip by slightly flexing each of the outer fingers, which allows good wrist movement. It's also very good on sloping holds where friction is essential, because of the large contact area of skin with rock.

Some people find this grip position to be their strongest, while others struggle with it. However, since there is ultimately less skin in contact with the hold than with four fingers, grip/friction can be a limiting factor on certain holds. And, unsurprisingly, this grip type tends to work less well for climbers who have sweaty fingers!

This is quite a passive grip type, and on steep terrain it's not always that useful as you can't get your fingers into the back of the holds to help you pull inwards as well as downwards.

FOUR-FINGER OPEN HAND (PASSIVE)

With the four-finger open hand grip, the index finger is straight, the middle two fingers are bent at the PIP joint and the pinkie is straight. This grip type is often favoured by people who have a relatively short index finger compared to their middle two fingers. It's mechanically pretty strong since there is limited bend in the fingers.

Everyone's hands are different. We all have hold types and grip positions that we find naturally easier or harder to use. Some of us are great on slopers, while others favour crimps. Relative finger length will play a role in which grip types we prefer because our fingers will sit more comfortably in certain positions. Generally speaking, we are strongest when our wrist is relatively straight, and so we'll probably prefer to hold on with a grip position which keeps our wrist as straight as possible.

Let's take a look at the grip types and finger positions that we come across while climbing and training.

FOUR-FINGER OPEN HAND.

HALF CRIMP.

This grip type does not tend to work well if the index and middle finger are similar lengths. In this case, the wrist must bend outwards in order to keep the index finger straight. This results in a weird wrist angle, and reduced strength through the system.

This grip type is really good for simply hanging from edges, but it tends to be a bit limited in real-world climbing situations as the wrist can't move much around the hold. It's also difficult to really pull inwards on steep terrain with this grip type.

HALF CRIMP (QUITE ACTIVE)

With a half crimp grip, there is a 90-degree angle – or as close to this as the fingers will go – at the PIP joint of the index finger and middle two fingers. The pinkie will be straight. If you have a shorter pinkie, you will require more bend in your front three fingers to get the pinkie on the hold.

The half crimp is probably the most commonly used grip type. I'm not sure if this is because most people's finger lengths lend themselves to this grip type, or whether the predominance of comfy first-joint edges at indoor climbing walls in recent years has led to people favouring this grip type.

It's a bit more relaxed than a full crimp, but it provides most of the advantages of a crimp grip. It allows for good mobility around the hold as you climb: slightly adjusting the angle of your front three fingers allows you to move your wrist in all directions while maintaining a good grip on the hold.

However, when compared to the crimp grip, it doesn't allow you to pull outwards as much on steep terrain.

CRIMP (ACTIVE)

The crimp is essentially the same as the half crimp, but the pinkie will also be bent at about 90 degrees at the PIP joint. There is also likely to be more flex in the PIP joints, and the muscles in the palm will be more engaged. A lot of people crimp holds with a straight pinkie – if your pinkie is very short relative to your front three fingers, you may do the same.

The crimp grip gives you a lot of control of handholds, instead of relying heavily on friction. It allows you to move your body around a really solid platform and pull in multiple directions on a hold, rather than just dangling below it.

Because your fingers are all wrapped up, you can actually gain a little bit of reach off a full crimp when you're stretching upwards – but you can lose a bit on a wide span move. I personally think the full crimp is the strongest and most useful grip for most climbing situations. Which is a shame because I find it desperate!

FULL CRIMP.

Because of the acute angle at the DIP joints when crimping, you put a lot of mechanical load through your joints and pulleys. Crimping is generally considered to be the most risky grip type for causing finger injuries, but I think this is exactly the reason that you should train it, rather than avoid it in your training (see chapter 8)!

FULL CRIMP (VERY ACTIVE)

The full crimp is the same as the crimp, but with the addition of the thumb wrapped over the index finger. Personally, I prefer to do the bulk of my fingerboard crimp training without

CRIMP.

my thumbs as this is a lot friendlier on my index fingers (I often tear my index finger cuticles when I wrap my thumbs over). I do, however, use a full crimp when I'm training on a board or climbing. In these situations, it feels like the diversity of hold types used is likely to cause less wear and tear on the skin of the index fingers.

FINGER COMBINATIONS

As well as these standard grip types, there are also different possible combinations of fingers:

/ Front three
/ Back three
/ Front two
/ Middle two
/ Back two
/ And all the individual fingers as monos

These can be used in an open position or in one of the crimp positions.

FINGER FORM

When it comes to training, form is crucial. It's worth bearing this in mind when you are on a fingerboard – or climbing, or doing any other type of training. Simply getting through your sets any which way you can isn't necessarily going to yield improvements in the right areas.

As an example, let's imagine you're training your crimp strength. If on your last couple of sets your fingers drop into an open-handed

position, there's no point continuing the hang as you are no longer targeting the desired finger position. You would be better off reducing the load and ensuring that your form is perfect for all sets, rather than going full beans and just about scraping through the exercises with bad form.

When training a specific grip isometrically (with static hangs), you will only gain strength at about +/- 15 degrees of that joint angle. If your fingers fall out of position by more than 15 degrees, then you will no longer be training the grip which you set out to train. This is why I don't believe the benefits of half crimp training necessarily cross over to full crimp training as well as people like to think.

Crimping can be quite unpleasant and as a result people often avoid it and default to a nice comfy half crimp instead. Sadly, though, to get better at crimping, you've got to crimp!

I'm always strongest open handed. I feel good in a four-finger half crimp, but as soon as I get up into the full crimp position I don't feel as strong. This is great for training, however, as it means I can hang on a fairly large edge in a full crimp position and it feels hard. There's no need for me to add much weight to have a good workout, whereas if I'm hanging from both arms with a half crimp grip – a more open-handed position – I can have 60 kilograms dangling off me without too much of a problem. Which is literally a pain in the back!

FRONT THREE CRIMP.

BACK THREE HALF CRIMP.

FRONT TWO OPEN HAND.

MIDDLE TWO OPEN HAND.

BACK TWO HALF CRIMP.

MONO – OPEN HAND.

As mentioned before, Shauna has small, strong fingers which seem to fit really well on to small handholds. She very rarely has to full crimp anything. Fingery climbing just never feels that hard for her – she can casually hold on in a half crimp position and, as a result, she's never had to really train the full crimp grip. She also rarely open-hands holds as it's more painful on her skin than half crimping. The majority of her training therefore revolves around half crimping as it's the most useful for her climbing.

FINGER MORPHOLOGY

As I said earlier, everyone's fingers are different. Different lengths, different thicknesses, bony and thin, fat and podgy, sweaty, dry ...

Generally, those with particularly short index fingers will tend to favour an open-handed gripping position rather than a half crimp. People with a short pinkie relative to their other fingers will tend to favour three-finger crimping as their pinkie struggles to get in the mix.

It's worth figuring out what your body naturally favours when it comes to holding on to handholds. Then you can find ways of working your weaker areas, which should help you improve your overall finger strength and potentially reduce the chance of future injuries.

SKIN

Our skin is the interface between our bodies and the climbing surface, whether it's rock, resin or wood. It's important that we understand how it behaves when we climb or train. We need to be prepared to take good care of our skin if we want to optimise it for climbing.

Different people have different skin types on their fingers. Some people have hard, dry skin which can split and crack easily, but is often great for rock climbing as it doesn't sweat a lot. Others have soft, sweaty skin which rarely splits, but can be frustrating for climbing as the sweat build-up causes them to slip off the holds, wearing down the skin quickly.

Women tend to have colder hands than men; it's harder to keep them warm, but they tend to sweat less. Some people have poor circulation, leading to cold hands and reduced sweating. Other people have good circulation which means warmer hands and usually more sweat, but also the ability to heal splits more quickly as the blood flow is so good. Their hands also stay warmer when it's cold outside.

As you can see, everyone is different. You need to figure out how your skin behaves under different conditions and adapt your training and – possibly more importantly – your climbing and skincare regimes accordingly.

SHAUNA DEMONSTRATING HER HALF CRIMP SKILLS.

Depending on hold material – the rock type, resin type or wood type – you might get more out of your skin if it's slightly softer and more moist (for example, with smoother hold textures) or harder and drier (rougher textures).

When it comes to training, if you have dry skin you may need to moisten it to soften it before getting on the fingerboard – assuming you're not mad, and aren't using a resin fingerboard. If you are a sweater, you may need to chalk up between every single hang. While skin and conditions generally won't stop you training, unless all of your fingers are split and bleeding, they may well alter the quality of a training session. And your skin will pretty much always affect your performance on the wall to some extent, as it's the bit of your body which is attaching you to the holds.

Summary

There are loads of ways of holding on to the same handhold. You are likely to favour certain gripping positions because of the morphology of your hands and fingers.

When training your fingers, you'll only make strength gains at around +/- 15 degrees of the joint angle that you are training.

Therefore, remember to train specifically, and target your chosen area of finger strength carefully for maximum gains.

Good form is essential.

Look after your skin. See also page 142.

FINGERBOARD EXERCISES

THE AUTHOR ON *COMPACT CULTURE*, SHEEP PEN BOULDERS, WALES.
© *SHAUNA COXSEY*

When it comes to strength training on the fingerboard, there are essentially two options:

1 Repeaters
2 Maximum hangs

But before we start hanging, we need to briefly look at *how* we hang.

FINGERBOARDING FORM

A lot has been written about upper body 'form' while fingerboarding – don't hang on straight arms, don't hang with bend in the arms, and so on. It seems like everyone has their own opinion. In my experience, as long as you maintain tension and stability in your arms, shoulders, back and core while you hang, and you don't just sag on to your skeleton, your form otherwise doesn't matter so much.

You should hang however you feel comfortable. The whole point of fingerboarding is to work the fingers as hard as possible, so make sure that your fingers – not your arms or shoulders – are the reason that you're failing when you're fingerboarding. If you have weaknesses in other parts of your upper body, then work on these separately, and focus entirely on your fingers when you're on the fingerboard.

REPEATERS

A mainstay of fingerboard training. The Beastmaker 2000 was designed around our love of this particular exercise. Repeaters train a little more towards strength endurance rather than outright strength.

With repeaters, you essentially hang a hold for a set time, then rest for a set time and repeat a number of times.

This is a good go-to exercise as it's relatively safe due to the low impact nature of each hang, but it is tiring.

Be very careful to maintain your form as you tire. The last few hangs can get a bit scrappy – this is the risky time for losing form and potentially getting injured. If in doubt, lower the intensity and increase the quality of your hangs.

You should adjust the intensity so you are really fighting on your last couple of hangs in each set, and you should aim to be failing on the sixth.

You can easily tweak the hang and rest time of your sets to alter the difficulty over time, for example hanging for 6 seconds and resting for 4 seconds, or even 5 seconds on, 5 seconds off. You can alternate between sessions or blocks of shorter hang times and longer hang times to help keep your fingers on their toes.

EXERCISE	Repeaters
GOOD FOR	Strength/strength endurance
DESCRIPTION	Hang for 7 seconds, rest for 3 seconds. This is one rep. Six reps = one set and takes 1 minute.
SETS	One or two sets per grip type. Up to three grip types per session is enough.
REST	5 minutes between sets.
PROGRESSION	More/less hang time/rest per set, e.g. hang for 6 seconds, rest for 4 seconds. Add weight. Add sets per grip type. Use smaller holds.
HOW LONG FOR	I think you should always be training finger strength to some degree. Cycle between finger training methods throughout the year to keep your body on its toes. Repeaters are relatively safe as they're low impact.
WHEN	Always train strength when you're well rested and fresh.

DAVE PARRY ON *HADES LAIR*, LAD STONES, ENGLAND.
© *JOHN COEFIELD*

MAXIMUM HANGS

Aka max hangs. These are a very time-efficient way of improving finger strength. They are a little bit riskier in terms of injury than repeaters because the intensity of each hang is very high, but they are great for working the shorter and more immediate end of strength. I find it easy to measure progress with max hangs as they are so utterly simple, even if progress might seem slightly slower than with repeaters. Form is crucial!

You should be fully warmed up before doing max hangs. I build up the weight slowly, beginning with body weight and then adding weight, until I reach my maximum weight. Shauna seems to warm up for max hangs much faster than I do. We're all different. So make sure you listen to *your* body. Bear in mind that your session is likely to feel different from day to day. Personally, I like to finish my warm-up with a short hang at my maximum weight. This way I know that when I begin my max hangs, I am ready to hold on as hard as I possibly can.

When training max hangs, and once you are fully warmed up, I don't think there is any need to do more than five hangs per grip type. Just three max hangs can be enough, and this won't leave you feeling too tired if you're planning on climbing soon afterwards. Their maximal nature will stimulate your body to adapt without you having to load it over and over again.

The beauty of max hang training is that it can be done very quickly. Warm-up and max hangs on a few grip types can take as little as 30 minutes. Once you get used to it, it won't leave you exhausted. This type of session is great for adding to the beginning of your climbing session, or as a first session of the day. You can also get away with doing this session fairly often. With finger training, little and often is always better than a marathon session once a week (or less!).

Really concentrate on putting maximum effort into your hangs. It can feel quite unpleasant to try really hard on small holds, or to have loads of weight hanging from you, but bear in mind that for most of your session you'll be resting. So, when it comes to the exercise itself, try your absolute hardest.

Max hangs can be split into shorter-duration hangs of 5 to 12 seconds, and longer-duration hangs of around 20 seconds. There are also tendon hangs – longer still.

SHORT MAX HANGS

Short max hangs tend to focus on neuromuscular gains. This means that your muscles will adapt to use more of their muscle fibres more efficiently and output more strength as a result.

Hang for at least 5 seconds and for up to 12 seconds. The reason for the vague time is that you are likely to vary a fair bit between sessions: it's unrealistic to suggest 'hang for 10 seconds' and expect that to be your absolute maximum at any given load over a number of sessions. Provided you're in the 5 to 12 seconds range, it's going to work. There's no need to hang for longer than 12 seconds as after this point your muscles will have already recruited all possible muscle fibres.

While I find it easy to plateau with short max hangs, I do come back to them from time to time for a number of sessions (around ten) before going back to longer hangs.

EXERCISE	Short Max Hangs
GOOD FOR	Strength: neuromuscular gains
DESCRIPTION	Hang for 5 to 12 seconds. This is one rep. Three to five reps = one set.
SETS	One set can be enough, or repeat for up to five grip types.
LOAD	Adjust the load so 5 to 12 seconds is the absolute maximum you can achieve.
REST	2 to 3 minutes between each hang, or as long as you need so you can give 100 per cent effort again.
PROGRESSION	Add weight. Use smaller holds. One arm instead of two.
HOW LONG FOR	I think you should always be training finger strength to some degree. Cycle between finger training methods throughout the year to keep your body on its toes.
WHEN	Always train strength when you're well rested and fresh.

LONG MAX HANGS

Long max hangs are geared towards increasing muscle size and strength in the forearm which leads to slower but potentially longer-lasting gains in strength.

TENDON HANGS

Hanging for even longer can increase tendon stiffness, which increases contact strength – the ability to grab on really fast – as there's less give in the tendons. It's also good for the general health of your connective tissues.

EXERCISE	**Long Max Hangs**
GOOD FOR	Strength: muscle size and longer-lasting gains
DESCRIPTION	Hang for 20 seconds. This is one rep. Three to five reps = one set.
SETS	One set can be enough, or repeat for up to five grip types.
LOAD	Adjust the load so 20 seconds is the absolute maximum you can achieve.
REST	3 to 5 minutes between hangs, or as long as you need so you can give 100 per cent effort again.
PROGRESSION	Add weight. More hangs per grip type. Use smaller holds. One arm instead of two.
HOW LONG FOR	I think you should always be training finger strength to some degree. Cycle between finger training methods throughout the year to keep your body on its toes.
WHEN	Always train strength when you're well rested and fresh.

EXERCISE	**Tendon Hangs**
GOOD FOR	Contact strength and tendon health
DESCRIPTION	Hang for 30 to 45 seconds. This is one rep. Three reps = one set.
SETS	One set per grip type; up to three sets in total.
LOAD	Adjust the load so you fail at about 45 seconds.
REST	5 minutes between hangs.
PROGRESSION	Add weight. Use smaller holds.
HOW LONG FOR	I think you should always be training finger strength to some degree. Cycle between finger training methods throughout the year to keep your body on its toes.
WHEN	Always train strength when you're well rested and fresh.

THE AUTHOR ON *JACK'S BROKEN HEART*, MAGIC WOOD,
SWITZERLAND. © *SHAUNA COXSEY*

ONE ARM OR TWO?

Any fingerboard exercise can be performed
on one arm or two arms.

Two-arm hangs are great as you can pretty
much guarantee that the weak link in the
chain will be your fingers, rather than your
arms or shoulders. The reason you will fatigue
and fail at an exercise is because your fingers
are getting worked, not because some other
part of the system is struggling.

One-arm hangs are great for climbers whose
arms and shoulders are strong enough that
they can perform them. You can put a lot of
load through your fingers, without having to
hold on to really small holds.

PICK UP WEIGHTS TO TRAIN ONE- OR TWO-FINGER GRIPS.

Be aware that training on one arm is only useful if your shoulders and arms are strong and stable enough to support you throughout the exercise. If you can't lock off on one arm on a bar or jug for the same amount of time as your fingerboard exercise, then I wouldn't recommend fingerboarding on one arm. This is simply because you're more likely to fail at the exercise because of fatigue in your arm or shoulder, rather than your fingers – even if you are using assistance with the free arm to remove some weight.

FURTHER EDGE-U-CATION …

I have covered the main fingerboard exercises on the previous pages. These are performed by hanging your body weight (and sometimes extra or reduced weight) from a set of holds. If you want to work a much weaker grip type, or you don't have access to something that you can hang from, then another option is to simply pick something up.

Get yourself an edge and attach it to a small piece of plywood – or there are plenty of dedicated products now available on the market – and use this to pick up some weights from the floor, using the standard finger strength training methods above – repeaters, max hangs or tendon hangs – and your chosen grip types.

This system can be very useful for training one- or two-finger grip positions nice and gently, for warming up at the crag, or for training when you're on the road without access to a fingerboard.

Summary

Fingerboarding is simple. You have two main options:
1 Repeaters: a set of back-to-back hangs and rests.
2 Max hangs: hanging on really hard for a period of time.

You can adjust the intensity using a variety of methods including hold size, hang time and rest time. See *Fingerboard Variables* overleaf for more options.

With fingerboard training, little and often is much more productive than the occasional marathon session. Train your fingers all year round.

SHAUNA COXSEY ON *NAMASTE*, VÄSTERVIK, SWEDEN. © *NED FEEHALLY*

Fingerboard Variables

There are an almost infinite number of ways of tweaking your fingerboard workout to vary exactly how it loads and fatigues your forearms. If you feel like the gains from your current fingerboarding routine have started to plateau, you can mix it up and introduce something new or different. This will provide your body with an evolving set of stressors to adapt to, as well as preventing you from getting bored.

To increase the difficulty of a deadhang, you can:

/ Use a smaller hold
/ Hang on for longer
/ Add weight
/ Use fewer fingers
/ Hang from one arm instead of two
/ Rest for less time between sets

To decrease the difficulty of a deadhang, you can:

/ Use a bigger hold
/ Hang on for less time
/ Remove weight with a pulley set-up/ resistance band/foot on a chair, and so on
/ Rest for longer between sets

Generally, varying the angle of an edge rather than its size doesn't really work.

You start to rely more and more on friction, rather than strength. And due to variations in your skin, the conditions, the temperature and so on, this can lead to unpredictable sessions.

Using smaller and smaller holds is a good way to train. You can easily see and track progress. However, as the holds start to get really small, the conditions, the temperature, your skin condition and general finger morphology all start to add inconsistency into your hangs. With less skin in contact with the holds, it takes a smaller amount of moisture to make you slip.

Very small holds also tend to be quite painful. This is fine for the odd session, but trying to do session after session on six-millimetre edges can really start to hurt. Don't be limited by pain and skin! This is a great argument for varying your fingerboard sessions regularly: cycle through sessions of larger holds on one arm, larger holds with added weight, and smaller holds with no added weight (or weight taken off).

You can still stick to your chosen exercise – repeaters, max hangs – but just alter the apparatus (and of course the exact timings, weight, reps and sets will have to be tweaked too). This way you can continue to train consistently while keeping your skin in the best possible condition.

INCREASE THE DIFFICULTY WITH SMALLER HOLDS.

TACTICS PART 2

Chalk tips, plus a bit more on hand and skin maintenance. See pages 42 and 142 for more.

CHALK

Chalk is obviously great for improving friction, but if the layer of chalk is too thick then the chalk particles can slide over each other, almost creating a lubricant. Apply chalk, rub it into your hands and brush off the excess before pulling on. You'll get better grip and the holds will require less cleaning afterwards. Don't let chalk build up on the holds. It clogs the texture of the rock, usually reducing friction. Brush technology these days is great – there's no excuse for not cleaning the holds properly. This goes for rocks and indoor climbing.

CHALK TYPES

I really rate Friction Labs chalk. It's the first chalk which has been chemically tweaked with creating maximum friction in mind. It feels very grippy on my skin and seems to work way better on smoother textures such as limestone, quartzy Font and Rocklands style sandstones, resin and especially wood. I use small bags of it, rather than opening one big bag and letting it sit and absorb moisture over time – which is more of a problem in the humid atmosphere of the UK than in some other parts of the world. As soon as the rock has some bite to its texture, such as gritstone, I find that the type of chalk has less impact on grip. Experiment and find the chalk that works best for your skin type, and the conditions you're climbing in. I heard a story that Dai Koyamada carries three different bags of chalk. A damp one for ultra-low humidity days, a very dry one for high humidity conditions, and a bag that is somewhere in between. It sounds ridiculous, but why spend all your free time and money travelling somewhere to climb up rocks, and then not make the most of your opportunity?

TAPING

Work out a good taping method for splits and other skin issues. Superglue helps here (see overleaf). And make sure you use a high-quality tape, not a weak, spongy tape which will wear out and rip as soon as it comes into contact with the holds. Alex Megos showed me his ultimate taping method (see opposite). I've seen Alex climb after taping up most of his fingers – before taping, his fingers looked like a murder scene! After the (enormous) tape job, he was good to go and had a massive training session. This isn't for everyone, but a good tape job can salvage a session.

SPLITS

If you get a split, trim off any excess or flappy skin. Once you have finished climbing, wash your hands thoroughly, apply antiseptic cream and tape over the top. Once the split is close to healing you should let it dry out and sand away any rough skin. After the initial healing, sand back as much of the surrounding skin as possible to even out the skin to a smooth finish. I usually tape up splits for a few sessions even when they are healed as they always have a tendency to re-split along the original line of weakness.

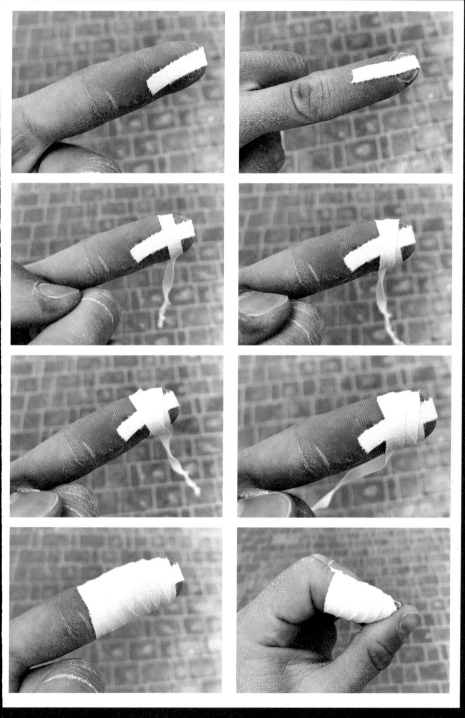

SHAUNA COXSEY ON *ZOMBIE NATION*, ALBARRACÍN, SPAIN.
© *NED FEEHALLY*

SUPERGLUE

Superglue (cyanoacrylate) has been a go-to for climbers for years. It's used for medical purposes – instead of stitches in small wounds and so on – so it definitely works. I use it mostly for gluing tape on to my fingers, and also for sealing pesky cuticle splits or gluing my fingernail down if I split underneath it (ouch). As well as the standard version which sets hard, you can get a rubberised version which sets to a slightly flexible consistency. I prefer the rubberised version for holding tape on and for sealing wounds as it moves slightly more with my fingers and it

cracks less. Superglue reacts with water so I find that breathing or blowing on it can help it to go off faster. Of course, cyanoacrylate is an irritant and it will bond your skin to anything in seconds, so I wouldn't recommend you lather yourself in it. And, also, if you have a tube in your climbing bag, keep it in a tin, box or plastic bag to prevent it from squirting all over your gear.

A trick which helps seal cuticle splits, or splits on a non-gripping part of a finger, is to dab glue over the wound, and then apply a thin

layer (a single ply) of tissue paper on to the glue. Allow this to dry and rub off the excess non-glued paper. The paper provides a fibrous matrix for the glue to bond to which I find helps it to keep the split closed for longer. Be prepared to re-tape and glue multiple times throughout a session for optimal performance. Tape is never as grippy as skin, so cover the absolute minimum of your skin that you can get away with while still covering the split, hole or cut.

HAND WARMERS

Great on really cold days. Keep them in your shoes when you're climbing and keep your climbing shoes in your pockets next to them when you're resting. These days you can get rechargeable USB hand warmers which last a few hours and kick out a lot of heat. You can also charge your phone from them!

SHOULD I TRAIN FULL CRIMPED?

Should I train full crimped?

It's often said that training full crimped is 'dangerous'. But, in my opinion, it's really important to train the full crimp grip position because a lot of hard moves on rock revolve around crimping really hard on small holds. You want to be ready for this when you go climbing for two reasons: first, you'll be stronger and better adapted to it, and second, it will minimise your risk of injury.

Don't be shy of the crimp.

HALF VS FULL CRIMPING

Half crimp training alone cannot fully prepare you to crimp with all your might on a tiny edge. Full crimping is a much more active gripping style than half crimping.

As discussed in chapter 4, full crimping is mechanically stronger than open-handing or half crimping when on small holds. The flexion in the DIP and PIP joints means that the fingers are at an advantageous angle for

holding on as the levers are shortened. This finger position is partly achieved by flexion of the MCP joints further down the hand – this allows a more acute angle to be achieved in the PIP joints. The lumbrical muscles in the palm are responsible for this movement and for holding the hand in place so the fingers can work. Flexing these joints also brings the thumb closer to the index finger – so it can wrap over the top for added strength. The interossei also work to stabilise the fingers as they become more flexed.

Also consider that the increased flexion of these joints in the hand creates more tendon/pulley interaction when under load, further adding to gripping power.

Fortunately, training the full crimp in total control on a fingerboard is relatively safe – although it is not 100 per cent risk free. There is none of the movement around the holds or out-of-control swinging about on the fingers which you simply cannot avoid while climbing.

Only ever training in a half crimp or open-handed position and then expecting to be able to crimp to your maximum on a project seems like madness to me.

Fortune favours prepared fingers.

SHAUNA COXSEY ON *MERLIN'S BEARD*, TINTAGEL, ENGLAND.
© *NED FEEHALLY*

GETTING TO GRIPS WITH YOUR FULL CRIMP

A lot of climbers feel like they lack full crimp strength, or feel that crimping is so unnatural that they simply can't do it. Their fingers just uncurl into an open-handed position while they climb. Crimping isn't necessarily a natural or comfortable way to hold on to a handhold, so lots of climbers tend to avoid it and as a result are quite unfamiliar with and unpractised at it.

If this is you, then slowly building up to being able to hang in a full crimp position is likely to really help your climbing. I have seen a lot of quite experienced climbers who have

only ever open-handed holds and are totally unable to hang off a hold in a full crimp position. I know it's usually more comfortable to open-hand, but if you're serious about climbing as hard as you can, you absolutely have to be able to full crimp.

As discussed previously, full crimping requires strength in the lumbricals and interossei in the hand. If you're very unpractised with full crimping then you may have weakness in these muscles and building strength here is an important first step. To be honest, I think most climbers – crimpers or open handers,

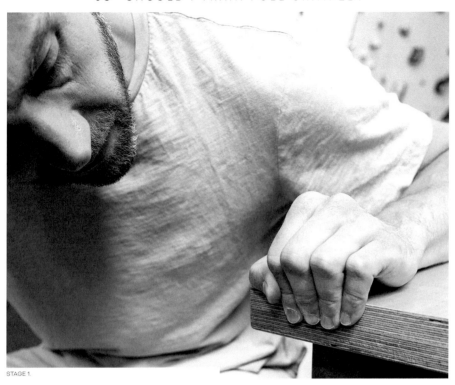

STAGE 1.

at every level of experience – should do some work on these muscles to keep their hands healthy and minimise the risk of injury. The health and condition of climbers' hands is often overlooked, which seems crazy given the punishment we put them through. We should look after our hands!

Check out *Hand & Upper Body Maintenance* (chapter 16) for some exercises you can do to help take care of your hands. These exercises should also help you to get your hand into a more advantageous position for crimping, and also hold it there while you crimp.

The next step is to get your body more used to having your hands in the crimp position. I recommend doing this in three stages.

STAGE 1
Grab hold of an edge – it could be the edge of a table, a door frame or a chair – and try to form a crimp grip with your hand: notice the position that your fingers naturally end up in.

Use your other hand to manipulate the crimping fingers into the full crimp position (all PIP joints, including the pinkie, at 90 degrees) while you pull gently on the edge of whatever it is that you're holding. At first this will feel very strange and may be slightly uncomfortable.

Repeat this over the course of a few days and weeks until your body becomes familiar with the position and your crimping fingers begin to naturally find the correct position.

STAGE 2.

Use a flat or slightly incut edge to encourage a crimp position, rather than a sloping edge which may cause the fingers to roll back into a more open position. Arm angle isn't really important, just try to keep your arm in a comfy position, not fully straight and not fully locked off, but somewhere comfortable in between.

STAGE 3

You should now be quite comfortable in the full crimp position, and able to notice when your form is good without having to constantly look at your fingers. Now is the time to get both hands involved at the same time.

Reduce the load accordingly, and slowly work up to being able to hold your body weight on two hands while maintaining the full crimp position.

You should now notice that when you're climbing, you're way more comfy on crimps, and hopefully a lot stronger.

From this point onwards you can start to train your crimp strength with all the usual fingerboarding exercises – max hangs and so on.

Summary

Don't be shy of the crimp – embrace it.

If you're new to or inexperienced with crimping, take care and build it up slowly.

STAGE 2

Let's start to introduce load, but first make sure you've done a good fingerboard warm-up and you're ready to pull hard!

Stand below a fingerboard or edge. Grab the edge in the full crimp position and gradually start to pull on it. **Keep your feet on the ground!** Watch very carefully that your fingers maintain their form. Simply stand and pull for 10 seconds per hand, as hard as you can while maintaining form. Perform about five sets per hand with plenty of rest in between.

Over a few sessions you should see a pretty big improvement in how hard you can pull while maintaining a solid crimp position in the fingers.

STAGE 3.

PINCHING

NARROW AND WIDE PINCH BLOCKS.

Most modern indoor training lends itself to developing good pinch strength as most bolt-on, screw-on and wooden holds tend to stick out from the wall, so usually offer somewhere for your thumb to oppose your fingers. This is great, as being able to pinch really hard seems like it should only be a good thing.

TRAINING PINCH STRENGTH

However, I have found that outdoors, pinches aren't as common a hold type as edges. I have never been amazing at pinches, and because I can't think of many climbs that I really want to do that revolve around pinches, I don't worry too much about training my pinch strength. However, I can see certain situations where amazing pinch strength would be very useful – such as competition climbing on volumes, hard tufa climbing and a lot of granite bouldering.

One thing I find with pinches, especially larger sizes, is that they are very often hand-size specific. If a pinch fits your hand it may well feel juggy, while for someone else who isn't able to get their thumb in the right place, it might feel impossible to hold.

One area that I have worked on a lot is narrow and small crimpy pinches. I have found that training on this style of hold has really helped my crimp strength, as the fingers are in the crimped position while the thumb is in opposition. This gripping style can be useful on rock, on closed seams or crimps in roofs where you can't wrap your thumb over the top.

> Shauna has tiny hands. She's very comfortable on small pinches but can find big pinches quite hard to use. As a result, she's spent a lot of time stretching her thumbs to increase their range and this has allowed her to get her hands around bigger pinches.

It's quite difficult to isolate pinch strength while climbing as you can often wriggle around pinches, rather than just engaging the thumb and squeezing. Turning a pinch into a sidepull is the classic way of avoiding the issue.

PINCH BLOCKS

Pick up weights with a pinch. This is a great way of isolating the hand and forearm muscles as you can't use any compression to hold on, just thumb squeeze. Whether the hand position alters the effectiveness remains to be seen, as when climbing you'll usually be pinching above shoulder level, and when picking up a pinch it's below shoulder level.

Pinch block training is definitely a useful method of developing pinch strength – it's simple and it's measurable. Treat the pinch block like you would a standard fingerboard exercise – pick up and hold a certain amount of weight for a particular length of time.

Also, use a pinch block that's the correct size for the size of pinch you want to work on and train. Remember the 15-degree joint angle rule (see page 66). You'll only gain strength at about +/-15 degrees of the joint angle that you're working on. Training with a huge fat sloping pinch won't help you if your project involves holding on to a really skinny pinch where all your fingers are basically in a crimped position.

PINCHING ON A BOARD.

PINCHING ON A BOARD

Making up boulder problems that use pinches on a board has always been my favourite way of training pinch strength. Providing you use footholds which mean you can't just turn each pinch into a sidepull or layaway! And also providing you make up problems where you have to actually pinch the holds in order to climb the problem. You'll know if you're cheating yourself. Remember that training isn't supposed to be easy.

As a rule, narrow moves will force you to engage your thumbs more, while wide pinch moves will encourage you to layback the hold rather than squeezing it. The angle of different pinches can also affect how good or bad they feel. If you're training for a particular route or boulder problem which features a pinch or pinches, aim to train on pinches which are as similar (size, shape and angle) as possible.

PINCHING ON A FINGERBOARD.

PINCHING ON A FINGERBOARD

The fingerboard can be a good place to train pinches, provided the pinches on your fingerboard are well suited. With parallel pinches, gripped with your thumbs facing towards you, you can use a lot of compression to hold on, rather than thumb strength. The gripping surface of the pinches should be horizontal rather than vertical to negate this effect, and ensure the thumbs have to squeeze for you to maintain grip.

Summary

When training pinch strength, be specific – if your project features a skinny, crimpy pinch, don't train for it with wide pinches.

BOARD TRAINING

THE KILTER BOARD. © *KEVIN TAKASHI SMITH/KILTER*

WHAT IS A BOARD?

And why is a board not a climbing wall, and vice versa?

A board is a top-end strength training device, while a climbing wall is a surface to climb on in an array of styles and at an array of difficulties.

The first training boards were built in small spaces – such as tiny British cellars – in the 1980s, at a time when climbing walls didn't really exist. They tended to be built by the very keenest climbers who had no other training options at the time, apart from going rock climbing or doing a few pull-ups on a door frame.

Climbers would build a short, steep climbing surface and cover it in loads of really bad handholds. The whole point of a board was that it was steep and hard, and it really packed a lot of difficulty into a small space. In this way, it was very useful to its users who had a load of hard moves to go at, even on a tiny climbing surface.

Since then, commercial climbing walls have appeared, and these days we have a mind-bending array of climbing surfaces, hold types and move types available at our local climbing walls.

Amongst all of this, the simple training board still has its place – our home training boards play a big role in mine and Shauna's training – and boards play a huge part in pushing standards in climbing today.

WHY TRAIN ON A BOARD?

Climbing usually involves reaching between handholds with our feet on the rock. Therefore, it makes sense that in order to improve at this – and therefore become a better climber – we should train by replicating it, but in the most difficult and focused way we can. Boards are great for this because we are doing climbing-related movements, but the steepness, size of handholds and footholds, and size of moves can all be controlled and tweaked to keep the intensity high. We are almost creating a caricature of hard climbing, with the elements that make a normal climb difficult being accentuated. Boards are a great way to work our weaknesses, as we can easily focus on the hold types or moves which we struggle with, and we can keep the intensity suitably high for every move.

Some of you may be lucky enough to already have access to your own board – especially after the Covid lockdown chaos of 2020 and accompanying board building frenzy. If so, that's great news, but I know that it's not possible for everyone. If you have access to a board at a climbing wall, that's great too. And if you have a say on what that board is like, then that's even better.

You might be considering getting your own board now. You could go down the route of buying an off-the-peg, pre-designed and pre-set board, such as the Kilter Board. These have become very popular. You will have a huge selection of problems to go at and a virtual community to climb with. If you're tight for time, or motivation, or even a decent training scene, then this could work well for you.

There is definitely a benefit in trying to climb on other people's problems and on moves which you wouldn't tend to make up for yourself. However, there are also significant gains to be made by forcing yourself to climb on problems and moves that you have set to specifically address and work your weaker areas. It's hard on the ego, but good for your climbing!

This section is all about making the most out of whatever board you have access to. Throughout, I will assume that you want to become a well-rounded climber, as this is something which I always train towards. Many of the points that I make are with this in mind. Of course, if you are training for a very specific goal, or you have no interest in, for example, climbing on small crimps, then you can pick and choose the parts which apply to you.

WHY USE A BOARD OVER A STANDARD CLIMBING WALL?

These days climbing walls set so many interesting and inspiring boulder problems that surely we can just train on these? I'd argue that board training is much more geared towards increasing climbing-specific strength (small holds, big moves, steep angles, consistent difficulty and so on) than standard indoor problems which may revolve around some blobs, unusual moves or a slippery foothold.

Board training also helps to develop creativity. In order to make up problems, we really need to think about the moves and how different holds work relative to each other. Forcing ourselves to consider this is so useful for developing our understanding of climbing and is an element of training that I feel

BOARD DESIGN

can get missed out these days. People are getting spoon-fed a bit too much and aren't developing their creative and analytical climbing brains as much as folk used to when the training facilities weren't so good.

So, if you're lucky enough to be able to build your own board, how should it be designed, or how can you make the most of an existing board? If you already have access to a board, you could skip to page 115.

SIZE

It's not all about size, it's how you use it ...

A huge board may look impressive, but is it the most efficient use of space?

I find that boards in commercial walls are often too big to be useful. If you can't reach all the holds to clean them, or you can't pull on in any position, then I feel like the board's use starts to become limited. Why have a tall board when all your problems start standing and finish on a big hold two-thirds of the way up?

Boards are generally all about maximum strength training. You should stick to five moves or fewer for this style of training. If a board is too big and you end up doing six to ten moves – or, Heaven forbid, more than that! – per problem, then you can't focus purely on strength, as the intensity of each individual move can't possibly be high enough.

Of course, big boards have their place for circuits and strength-endurance training, but I think you are better off setting up a board for either all-out strength or endurance training, rather than doing a slightly poor job of combining both.

ANGLE

The angle of your board can depend on your goals and the space which you have available, but, generally speaking, the steeper the board, the bigger the holds will need to be. Steeper and shallower boards have their relative attributes and merits.

Steeper boards (≥45 degrees)
/ Less headroom needed to fit them in.
/ Generally bigger holds.
/ More weight on the upper body.
/ More tension required to keep the feet on.
/ Moves tend to be more 'dangly' than 'pully'.

OUR SIDE-BY-SIDE BOARDS ARE DESIGNED TO TRAIN OUR SPECIFIC NEEDS. © *BAND OF BIRDS*

Shallower boards (30–45 degrees)

/ Can have a smaller footprint than a steep board, so may fit better in a small room.
/ Can use smaller handholds which is potentially more rock specific.
/ More pully in the arms.
/ Can do longer circuits more easily, should you want to.

Crucially for many home board builders, shallower-angled boards require more headroom, so often they just won't work in a standard room of a house or in a garage. For example, a three-metre-long climbing panel at 45 degrees would be just over two metres tall, while the same panel at only 30 degrees would need an additional half a metre of headroom.

The biggest disadvantage of shallower-angled boards for strength training is that your feet can do a lot of the work, even with small or poor footholds. In addition, you will usually need to have incredibly small

handholds to make the moves hard enough, which can become quite unpleasant after a while – skin should never be a limiting factor in your training if you can possibly avoid it. If a board is shallower than 30 degrees, you will probably be pulling on such tiny holds it will be horrible! I'd avoid this if you have any regard for your skin.

In a perfect world, you would have access to a number of boards of various angles, with different styles of holds on them. But this isn't realistic for most of us. If you're building your own board, you'll have to decide on an angle. This will partly be dictated by the dimensions of the space that you have.

I built my first board at 56 degrees. This was mainly so I could fit it in a basement with a low ceiling. Fortunately, I think this is a great angle for my training. The holds tend to be (but aren't exclusively) fairly large – generally around first joint or larger – which makes

them comfy for climbing on. However, they aren't especially incut and they have very little texture – this means I need to maintain good body tension and a whole lot of squeeze in my hands in order to link any moves. My board is a top-end strength-training device; for anything less intense I go to a commercial climbing wall. For the highest-intensity moves in a style which will really benefit my climbing, my board fits me perfectly. My advice is that you consider what you would like your board to do for your climbing.

Since building my first board I have been able to build another board next to it. This second board was geared more towards Shauna's training. It has bigger but less positive handholds coupled with more positive footholds. The idea is that Shauna can work on longer, extended moves, clawing in with her feet and training strength at maximum extension. Generally, if the holds are incut, she finds them

too easy! So I made a bunch of sloping handholds which require good body tension to hold on to and move around. Now we have two boards at the same angle, but which climb totally differently and develop totally different skill sets.

HANDHOLDS

If you have the luxury of your own board or access to a board that you have free rein over, then good for you. Make the most of it. Here are some things to think about with board handholds.

/ Painful skin caused by uncomfortable holds should never be a factor.
/ Limit the number of sharp and minging holds. A few can be useful, especially if you have goals that revolve around small, sharp crimps. But default towards nice comfortable holds, where possible. Unless you are one of the weirdos who likes yanking on razor-blade crimps.

/ Comfortable doesn't necessarily mean juggy. A difficult hold can also be comfy.

/ Nothing overly incut. Holds are much nicer if they are larger and less positive, rather than tiny and very incut.

/ Large radii on holds is almost always better.

/ Rounded is good, but round shapes can put sideways stress on your fingers.

/ Use wooden holds. If you must use resin, make sure the holds are quite smooth. Training sessions shouldn't be limited by your skin if you can possibly avoid it. I find that most resin holds are simply too rough to train on for any length of time. And, if they're smooth, they often feel slippery.

/ Wood is a porous material, so it soaks in sweat a little, while resin isn't porous and relies on the chalk in the texture to absorb your fingers' sweat.

/ Keep the holds clean! Chalk can build up over time, making the holds slippery. Use your rest time to clean off your chalk from your previous attempt.

/ Try to put on a load of holds which you find hard to use. Don't just pick out the holds that you like because you feel strong on them.

FOOTHOLDS

Different footholds can completely change the way a board climbs. You have three main options:

/ feet follow hands
/ separate positive/incut footholds
/ separate sloping footholds.

Each option has its advantages.

The **feet follow hands** approach makes for some interesting moves and will allow you to train a whole array of move types. Generally, this approach works on body strength and coordination as well as finger strength. You can work on heel hooks and toe hooks too, and learn to make the most of the holds which are available to you. This approach tends to work better on blobby resin holds rather than wooden holds and it is a great way to train. But, you must be careful to make up problems which work your weaknesses, as climbers often swing towards their usual or strongest move style when setting problems.

This is the classic 'spray wall' style of climbing. I think it's great, but it generally relies on a bigger board in a big facility to best accommodate it. Most home boards are simply too small to work well with this approach. Also, if you have a board with wooden handholds, you'll probably want to use specific footholds so that you don't ruin your lovely wooden holds by standing on them!

Separate positive/incut footholds will allow you to claw in and pull with your legs, training your whole body and building strength from the tips of your toes to your fingertips. With this style of foothold, you'll tend to do larger moves, and work strength which runs all the way down your body. Leg strength is incredibly useful in climbing, and is commonly overlooked. Moves on rock often revolve around leaving the feet low and getting stretched out, so it's worth training in this style.

POSITIVE/INCUT FOOTHOLD.

SLOPING FOOTHOLD.

Sloping footholds focus the training stimulus on the fingers, upper body and active core strength – pushing hard through poor footholds. The main footholds on my board are quite large but they are sloping and really not that helpful.

I favour sloping footholds for the bulk of my board training. This encourages me to apply pressure through my feet in order to keep them on the holds, which develops climbing-specific body tension. It also means I can set boulder problems which rely heavily on not cutting loose, so the crux is almost always keeping my feet on as I move. This feels very rock specific.

A secondary advantage of sloping footholds is that you don't have to rely on a decent edge on your shoes in order to stick to small positive footholds. This means you can train in any old floppy, worn-out comfy shoes rather than relying on your brand-new, expensive, toe-crushing shoes.

Shauna prefers to train on positive footholds, and especially footholds which are far away from the handholds. She's quite short (164.5 centimetres), so climbing for her often involves getting very spanned and stretched out between the handholds and footholds. She trains a lot at maximum extension so she can make the most of her height. As I mentioned above, 'her' board is set with sloping handholds coupled with positive footholds.

Ideally, you would have two or three specific sets of footholds on your board (in addition to any feet-follow-hands problems that you may have): sloping footholds, positive footholds, and a small selection of big 'juggy' footholds. The juggy footholds are good for warming up and for training really stretched out 'clawing in' moves – down low or out to the sides.

Different foothold options will allow you to get way more out of your board. The same handholds sequence will climb totally differently depending on which footholds you're using, giving you way more training options in a limited space.

HOLD LAYOUT

There are two main approaches to hold layout on boards. You can put a range of holds on at random. This will provide you with a load of move options. Or you can arrange the holds in a symmetrical pattern to create a mirrored board. This provides you with the opportunity to climb a boulder problem on one side and mirror it on the other side. Here are some things to bear in mind, whichever approach you take.

/ When first setting your board, try not to get carried away and instantly cover it in all your holds. This is a common mistake. You'll get much more out of it in the long run if you put a minimal number of holds on, climb on them and add holds when and where you need them. This system ensures you get the right spread of hold types and sizes across the board. Patience is key. I recommend starting with around 25 per cent of the total number of holds you'll eventually have on the board, and slowly adding more from there.

/ Have a few larger holds for getting going – they don't need to be full-blown jugs, as you can do most of your warming up off the board – and a good selection of medium and small holds in the gaps. Putting the larger warm-up holds around the edges of the board is a good idea as it keeps them out of the way of the main section of the board, so you'll be less likely to collide with them.

/ Depending on your goals, you'll want a range of different-sized edges, sidepulls and gastons, undercuts, pinches, and some pockets.

/ Add some holds that are big enough to match or even swap hands on comfortably (but not piano style!). Matching isn't a bad thing. Matching in close on a hold is a common move on rock so don't shun it because it's not cool. A good way of progressing is to do a problem with matching, then work towards doing it without matching.

/ Aim for a good spread of holds across the board. There's no point having all your crimps in one small corner of the board, or a load of undercuts at the top of the board. Be patient and set your board slowly, over a number of sessions, weeks and even

months, so that you can dial in what needs to be where. And don't be afraid to move things around as time goes by.

/ Think about handhold density – you will want to add a good number of holds to your board to maximise its useability. However, as soon as a board gets too cluttered, it may not climb as well. My main board is eight feet wide by 12 feet long (244x366 centimetres) and has about 130 handholds on it. If there were any more than this, I think the holds would start getting in the way of one other. I try to avoid having holds touching each other for two reasons: mainly because I prefer

the way this looks, but it also reduces the chance of colliding with the holds as I'm climbing.

/ Consider foothold density – don't overdo it. Have a couple of different foothold types spread across different areas of the board. My main board has 24 footholds: 12 Beastmaker chrome domes, and 12 wooden sloping footholds which I made myself. Too many footholds means too many options and too many foot moves per boulder problem, while not enough footholds leads to too many jumpy moves. Again, be patient, add slowly and find the balance.

OUR HOME BOARDS HAVE A SYMMETRICAL HOLD LAYOUT.

BOARD TRAINING

Even if you don't have your own board, but you're able to train on an existing board, consider the following:

REMEMBER: YOU'RE TRAINING

Remember that training on a board is training. It isn't about getting to the top however you can; it's about working on the areas you need to work on. If you feel like you would benefit from more body tension, then don't just campus up problems on the board. If you would benefit from better crimp strength, then don't just smash up on pinches because you're particularly good on them.

The same goes for the style in which you climb. If you find it easier to jump quickly between the handholds with your feet in minimal contact with the board, then perhaps you should try climbing more slowly and keeping maximal contact between your feet and the footholds per move or problem.

This seems like the most basic of concepts, but so many climbers get it wrong. Training is all about improving, by repeating something which you find hard until it becomes easy. It's not about showing off the things which you're good at.

KEEP IT SIMPLE ...

Board climbing is supposed to be basic. Reducing the complexity of the climbing movements means that what we are doing requires only maximum strength. Making our bodies work hard is the goal of board climbing. It's supposed to be physically challenging.

SYMMETRY?

The idea of symmetrical boards has been around for a while. Initially they were full-on system boards, with repetitive lines of holds running up them. Nowadays it has become common to see mirrored boards, which have a good spread of hold types, mirrored down the middle to enable the same set of moves to be climbed on each side, therefore training each side of the body equally. I prefer this mirrored style of board over a conventional random holds board. Routes and boulder problems on rock or indoors aren't symmetrical, so it isn't essential to train in this style, however it can be useful for a number of reasons:

/ The moves are replicated on both sides to train both sides of the body equally: this feels more like 'training' than climbing, which can be a nice thing.
/ It's a great way to identify and iron out any areas of unilateral weakness which you may have.
/ It's good for rehabbing injuries to see how your recovering side compares to your healthy side.
/ You get twice as much climbing out of each problem you make up.
/ Symmetrical boards look neat and tidy – very important!

I always try to climb each boulder problem on both sides. And I don't count it as an ascent unless I do both sides in a session.

Generally speaking, you should try to climb simply on a board. Avoid heel hooks, toe hooks and deep drop knees which take weight off your arms and fingers. You will be much better off practising these more complex movements at a commercial climbing wall or outdoors, where you have more space, a three-dimensional climbing surface and greater hold variety. Use the board for more simple strength training.

As with every other aspect of training, board climbing should be focused carefully on the areas which you need to improve. We all know a board climbing monster who has perpetually underachieved on rock. Always train with the bigger picture in mind, and **don't let your ego get in the way of a good session**.

... BUT CLIMB WELL

While board climbing is by its very nature not technical, that doesn't mean you must climb badly on a board. For example, if a foot move is the crux, don't jump past it: grind it out! You can make rules for your problems – eliminate certain footholds, no thumbs, three fingers only on a certain hold, use a different foothold to normal – in order to tweak the difficulty of what you're climbing on. But always concentrate on climbing well: don't just bully your way upwards to get the tick.

HANDHOLD TYPES AND MOVES

The great thing about climbing on boards is that you can work on a large variety of moves and handhold types in a very small space – providing the board has been set fairly well. You'll want a selection of bigger holds to get warmed up on, but beyond that you should maximise the amount of small/hard holds. **Tailor the board for your weaknesses and accept that you'll find it totally desperate.** While your mates may come along and cruise your hardest problems, you'll be the one who is improving in the long term. You'll learn much more from struggling to climb something which addresses your weaknesses than you will from doing something easily which suits your strengths.

PROBLEM STYLES

Climbers often enjoy using fairly large holds on boards and doing big moves between them. This is great fun, and I'm sure it helps their climbing to some extent, but realistically how many rock climbs revolve around doing only huge moves on incut holds? (OK, some do, but on the whole it's just not the case.)

WIDE MOVES.

NARROW MOVES.

I find it much more beneficial to train on problems with small and/or not incut/positive holds and to concentrate on doing smaller moves between them, focusing on the movement of the whole body. In my opinion you will get way more out of learning to climb between bad holds while maintaining tension than you will trying to do the biggest moves you possibly can on fairly large or incut holds. Of course, a bit of everything is useful, but the fashion these days seems to be for doing huge moves with your feet flying all over the place. I'm not convinced this has much use for rock climbing, as cool as it may look.

WIDE VS NARROW

Because of my build, I find narrow moves much harder than wide moves. Therefore I spend lots of time on my board working on twisting into narrow moves. Conversely, if you find wide or extended moves more difficult, then set yourself problems which work on this. As always, you should decide what exactly you need to train, and adjust your problems and sessions accordingly.

Shauna spends a lot of time on the board climbing at her full range. She finds small, bunched moves easy, but being short she benefits from climbing a lot at her maximum extension.

TWEAK THE DIFFICULTY WITH ANKLE WEIGHTS.

PROBLEM LENGTH

Think of individual moves like 'reps' when you're lifting weights, and the boulder problem as a 'set'. So, in terms of effort, a short boulder problem of three moves should feel like three maximum reps with a heavy weight.

As long as the moves you're doing are hard:

/ one to five moves will work maximum strength
/ five to 15 moves will work strength endurance
/ any more than 15 moves is full-on endurance training.

WEIGHTS AND ANKLE WEIGHTS
I've had a lot of success over the years training with ankle weights. They are a great way of tweaking the difficulty of problems when climbing on a board. If you have a few sets available, you can use them to easily mix things up and vary your sessions. I started with 0.5-kilogram weights (per leg), and have built up to now being able to climb some problems on my board with 5-kilogram weights (per leg). I think ankle weights work much, much better when you're climbing on the right kind of footholds – sloping or poor. If the footholds are too incut then the benefits are limited, although not entirely negated.

In my opinion, these are the advantages of ankle weights over a weight belt or vest:

/ less weight can be added for things to feel harder
/ they train foot precision as you must take way more care when placing your feet
/ they develop body tension and punish you when your feet cut
/ they don't get in the way as much as a vest or belt
/ they are light enough to easily transport between facilities
/ you can wear them stealthily under your trousers.

Some people argue that adding weight while you climb changes your centre of gravity and can teach you bad movement habits. There may be some truth in this, but I think that if you're at a point where you are thinking about adding weight while training on a board, then you are probably a fairly experienced climber. You have already learned a lot about movement and it will take many hours of climbing with added weight to upset your body's carefully tuned movement patterns. If you do have a few sessions with added weight and then instantly forget how to climb without the weight on, perhaps climbing isn't the sport for you!

Generally, added weight makes you try hard and therefore you learn how to try hard. A good way to have a really hard session is to pick a handful of problems on the board which are usually 75 to 95 per cent of your max. Add a couple of kilograms of weight (on the ankles ideally, or with a vest or belt) and try to complete these problems again, one after the other. You already know you can climb them, but you'll have to dig deep to get up them with the added weight.

Adding a bit of weight is a great way of mixing up a session if you want to change something but you don't want to make up any new problems. Add some weight, take your brain out and get on your normal circuit. Things will immediately feel a lot harder.

Overall, I think that adding weight is a very simple and useful way of changing the training stimulus. Just don't overdo it as it can be very intense on the body.

STRUCTURING YOUR SESSIONS

Training on a board isn't about getting to the top of the hardest problems all the time.

WARMING UP

Boards by their nature are very intense to climb on. Even relatively easy board problems are hard work for the body compared to rock climbs and normal problems at the climbing wall.

It's a good idea to try to get mileage in on a board, rather than only climbing on it when you feel amazing, and ticking off a project.

Aim to build yourself a warm-up circuit of five to ten problems (if you're on a symmetrical board, you should climb each problem on both sides), and then have a selection of projects in various styles that you can try after you have warmed up. If you climb your warm-up problems every session, then you'll always be getting some mileage out of your sessions.

Of course, the term 'warm-up' here isn't strictly accurate. I tend to warm up from cold off the board: that might be on the fingerboard and by doing pull-ups, or maybe even a session at a climbing wall. I'll then get on the board for my warm-up circuit. This starts with the easiest problems on the board and works its way up to some hard problems that are at about 80 per cent of my max.

I aim to have the difficulty of my warm-up circuit at a level where on a good day I can climb every problem first go, but on an average day I'll drop a couple of problems a couple of times. They shouldn't all be total paths! While I know that I can do them, I must try hard to get up them.

This approach to warming up is a great way of checking in on your body and seeing where you are at at the start of your session. It can help you to decide what to do with that session. If you plan to have a hard session, but then fall off more than normal during your warm-up circuit, maybe you shouldn't try to climb at your absolute maximum that day. Over time you'll become familiar with your warm-ups and you can adjust the remainder of your session according to how you feel.

To tweak the difficulty of your warm-up, you can:

/ rest for less time between problems
/ use poorer footholds or just different foothold placements to normal
/ add weight (a couple of kilograms at a time), or 0.5 kilograms at a time with ankle weights
/ do more problems in your warm-up phase
/ set some harder warm-up problems.

You'll find that at first your warm-ups will feel desperate, but over time they will become easier and easier until you have to drop the easiest ones and introduce some harder problems to your circuit.

SESSION INTENSITY

For a hard board session I try to work at a problem success to failure ratio of 50:50. So, with a warm-up circuit and some hard projecting, I will spend roughly 50 per cent of my climbing time getting up stuff, and 50 per cent trying really hard on projects. An easier board session will be about 75:25 success to failure – more time spent getting up stuff, with a sprinkling of projects on top.

I think the advantage of getting in some mileage during a board session is that your body becomes used to climbing on physically strenuous moves. If you only ever try projects at or above 100 per cent of your max, then you'll spend a lot of time sitting on the mats and very little time actually climbing with your muscles engaged. While projecting like this is good fun, I feel it has its limitations. Of course, throwing in the occasional session with projects at and beyond your max is good,

but in my opinion your average board session should involve at least a bit of mileage.

I will also sometimes have easy sessions where I just run through a warm-up circuit and then stop. This is basically the easiest possible session that I can do on the board. If I'm tight for time but I want to get moving, then it's easier for me to do this than it is to go to the wall and have a session there.

MY TYPICAL BOARD SESSION STRUCTURE

I normally do this two or three times a week, but it varies depending on factors such as how much outdoor climbing I've been doing, whether I have been busy with work, whether I am training for anything in particular, whether I have any injuries or tweaks that I am working around, and so on.

/ Fingerboard warm-up, building up to three or four max hangs to make sure my fingers are totally warm.

/ Start on my easiest problems and climb ten warm-up problems (on both sides as the board is symmetrical), alternating the style of footholds between sessions to keep things fresh.

/ Try a number of projects for roughly one hour, focusing on one or two areas – crimps, pinches, tension, shouldery moves, and so on.

/ Finish with a number of easier problems on decent-sized holds with ankle weights.

/ Stop, eat and stretch.

Shauna's typical sessions are generally more relaxed than mine – I think she finds climbing on boards easier than I do so she doesn't have to try as hard. She will normally start her warm up on the fingerboard, and then climb a circuit of five warm-up boulder problems on big footholds, followed by five warm-up boulder problems on small footholds. She uses this to gauge how she feels. If she's feeling good she will then climb on hard projects. If she's not feeling so good she will turn the session into a mileage session and climb a load of problems at about 50 to 70 per cent of her maximum. Her sessions last one to two hours, mainly depending on what other training she has already done or will do later that day.

KICKING FEET OFF ON EVERY MOVE.

TWEAKING YOUR BOARD SESSIONS

Here are a few ideas for how you can mix up your board sessions to keep things varied and interesting, and to ultimately keep you going back session after session.

/ Use different footholds to your usuals: force yourself to use wonky feet on your standard problems.
/ Add a bit of weight (on ankles or otherwise).
/ Adjust your success:failure ratio – add a few easier problems to your warm-up circuit for a mileage session, or add a few hard projects for a harder session.
/ Remember that 50 percent success to 50 per cent failure is a good ratio for a hard board session, but don't limit yourself to only this.
/ Link two easier problems together, either up and down, or by stepping off at the top and immediately getting on the second problem with no rest.
/ Limit rest.
/ Do not cut loose at all.
/ Kick feet off on every move.
/ Take feet off and hang for 3 seconds on every move.

Summary

Board climbing is great for training. It's almost as much fun as 'normal' climbing, but it's physically more strenuous, so it encourages strength gains in the important areas – finger strength, body tension and pulling strength.

Board climbing involves movement. Unlike more basic strength training methods – such as fingerboarding or other off-the-wall training activities – this movement element is highly relatable and transferable to climbing.

Board climbing encourages creativity – thinking about moves and making up problems. This element of training is so important, and can be missed these days with climbing walls taking a lot of the thought out of people's training.

Think of board training as the perfect combination of climbing and training.

Board climbing is supposed to feel physically hard! That's what makes it fun.

What can I do?

Climbing on a board is more intense than a standard climbing session. If you're new to boards, then make sure you take it steady.

Try to make up moves and problems which address your weaknesses – where you want to improve.

/ Try existing problems 'no thumbs'.
/ Lock off on each move. Reach to the next hold and hover your hand over it for 3 seconds before grabbing it and moving on. This will force you to slow your climbing pace. Board problems are often climbed very quickly, but locking the moves can help to slow your pace down so it more accurately replicates 'normal' climbing.

ENDURANCE TRAINING

ENERGY SYSTEMS

Over the last few years, a huge amount has been written about endurance training. It's easy to borrow the science from classic endurance sports like running and cycling and apply it to climbing, and it translates reasonably well. However, in spite of the similarities, training for climbing is bound to have some differences.

Climbing is not a linear sport – it requires intermittent bouts of effort separated by periods with much less effort. Also, climbing mainly uses smaller muscle groups than running and cycling, so it places much less demand on the cardiovascular system in general.

If you're really into sport climbing, or generally training endurance, you are likely to already know a lot more than is written in this chapter. I was unsure whether to include a section on endurance at all. In essence, training endurance is a bit dull, but it is very important – even for climbers whose primary focus is the strength side of the sport. More endurance will mean faster recovery between attempts on boulder problems, and will mean you can train harder for the things you really care about. So here is a *very* streamlined version to get you started, and hopefully not bore your socks off …

Climbing places different demands on our bodies depending on the intensity. When we do lots of really easy moves in a row, our forearms will use oxygen to create fuel (from carbohydrate, fat and protein). The oxygen and nutrients are delivered by our circulating blood. This circulating blood also removes the waste products that our muscles produce.

This **aerobic ('with oxygen') energy system** provides our forearm muscles with a small amount of energy, basically indefinitely. So, if we are climbing on sufficiently easy terrain, we can keep going for as long as we want without getting tired. And when we're resting between climbs or attempts on a climb, this system helps to refuel our muscles and remove waste products.

However, climbers like to try hard, and link loads of hard moves together. As the intensity of the moves increases and we are forced to hold on harder, our contracted forearm muscles squeeze our capillaries closed, limiting blood flow. In this case, oxygen cannot be used to provide fuel for the muscles, because it can't get to them. The muscles have to get their fuel from an internal source – their stores of adenosine triphosphate (ATP, a molecule which delivers energy to cells) and glucose.

This **anaerobic ('without oxygen') energy system** can provide a large amount of energy but for a finite amount of time. It's not entirely clear why, but for some reason the anaerobic energy system can only provide energy for a short time which is why after climbing a number of hard moves in a row we start to feel tired and eventually we can't hold on any longer.

For this streamlined take on climbing endurance, let's look at two parts of the anaerobic energy system:

The **anaerobic lactic system** uses glucose as fuel and produces lactate. This energy system can fuel us for around ten to thirty hard moves in a row before our muscles fatigue.

The **anaerobic alactic system** uses ATP as fuel. Using this system, our muscles can output their maximum force, but only for a very limited amount of time. One to five very hard moves in a row. This is essentially our maximum strength.

To summarise:

ENDURANCE TRAINING ON THE CIRCUITS BOARD.

ENERGY SYSTEM	SPEED OF ENERGY DELIVERY	FUEL SOURCE	DURATION	USE	CLIMBING EXAMPLE	SUMMARY
Aerobic	Slow	Oxygen plus carbohydrate/ fat/protein	All day	Low-intensity moves for a long time, and refueling muscles during rest	An easy, all-day multi-pitch climb	Long endurance
Anaerobic lactic	Fast	Glucose	20 seconds to 2 minutes	High-intensity moves for a short time	A ten-metre section of sustained hard climbing	Short endurance
Anaerobic alactic	Instant	ATP	<10 seconds	The hardest moves you can do	A steep, three-move boulder problem	Strength

Of course, there is overlap between these energy systems – during a normal climbing session our muscles will be getting fuelled by all three systems and different climbs will tax the different energy systems more or less.

Crucially, and quite simply, the more energy we use per move, the faster our fuel supplies will get depleted, and the faster we will get tired. So, if we can get stronger, fitter or both, we'll be able to do more hard moves in a row.

PRIORITIES

Different climbing goals require different skill sets. Personally, as a boulderer, I require a high level of strength and a decent level of short endurance for longer boulder problems. These longer problems will realistically be only up to 20 moves long, though – any longer and I probably wouldn't bother trying them! I find it incredible how fit sport climbers are. The idea of climbing hard moves all the way up a 30-metre (or longer) route, while recovering on marginal rests, just boggles my mind. Very impressive.

However, a fairly well-developed aerobic/long endurance energy system is useful for me as well because it can help me recover between attempts on boulder problems. Of course, I don't put as much time into endurance training as I could or should, but I'll usually do a block of long endurance training once a year, either because I feel like I need a change from very high-intensity climbing and training, or because I'm going away on a climbing trip where I know I'll be trying to climb all day

and will want to recover effectively between boulder problems.

> Shauna's training for the combined format at the Olympics involved preparing to compete in bouldering, lead and speed. As a result, she needed to be as strong as she could be for the bouldering, while also having very high levels of short endurance as competition lead climbs are generally 30 to 40 moves long with few rests. She also needed to be able to recover quickly between events, so a high level of long endurance was crucial. So she spent countless hours on the wall or fingerboard training her short and long endurance. It was incredibly tedious, but she's very stubborn. Sorry, I mean she's an athlete, and that's why she's so good!

You need to figure out where your endurance priorities lie, and train accordingly.

/ One- to five-move boulder problems require little endurance.
/ Five- to 20-move boulder problems or short routes require a lot of short endurance.
/ Routes with 60 moves upwards generally require mostly long endurance.

But, of course, there are all sorts of lengths of climbs that all fit somewhere on a spectrum of requiring maximum strength or endless aerobic endurance. And, more often than not on sport routes, a bit of both as there will be distinct crux sections which are separated by rests.

JULES LITTLEFAIR ON *THRILLER*, MALHAM COVE, ENGLAND. © *STU LITTLEFAIR*

HOW DO I TRAIN ENDURANCE?

In practical terms, if you want to get 'fitter' you have four options:

1 Climb more efficiently/quickly and so use less energy per move. Of course, this won't actually make you any fitter, but you will fatigue more slowly as you climb.

2 Get stronger. If each move requires a smaller percentage of your maximum strength, you'll be able to do more moves in a row.

3 Gain long endurance.

4 Gain short endurance.

This book isn't intended to teach you how to move more efficiently – sorry! And the rest of the book is designed to help you to get stronger. Which leaves training long endurance and short endurance.

LONG ENDURANCE

To train your long endurance, do a large volume of climbing at a low intensity – no more than 40 per cent of your maximum intensity. This will mean climbing for 15 to 20 minutes non-stop on very easy terrain, and resting for a long time between bouts of climbing.

Work on a 1:1 work:rest ratio – so if you're climbing for 15 minutes, rest for 15 minutes – and at around a pump level of 3/10, where 0/10 would be no feeling of pump at all and 10/10 would be failure. Try doing up to three bouts of this kind of climbing per session. Training long endurance like this is fairly

simple, but it is quite tedious. You're basically plodding on easy moves without ever doing anything as exciting as a crux move.

This training method causes a number of adaptations in your forearms; the main one is growing capillaries which in turn provide more pathways to deliver oxygen and fuel to your muscles.

Because long endurance training like this is quite low intensity, you can easily fit it in around other training. I do it *after* another training session of some sort, such as after a bouldering or fingerboard session. But definitely *not before* any kind of strength training. You can do it a couple of times a week without it really affecting your other training.

To notice decent gains in your long endurance you need to do a block of at least eight weeks of training for it. Aim for around two hours of long endurance training per week – either all together in one marathon session (very tedious) or split up over a number of shorter sessions (emotionally much more forgiving). You can do more than two hours per week if endurance is your priority, but it will probably start to impact upon your other climbing or training if you do much more than this.

SHORT ENDURANCE

You have a few options for training short endurance, but generally speaking you need to do much less volume than with long endurance training, but at a much higher intensity – around 70 per cent of your maximum intensity.

JULES LITTLEFAIR ON *LOS VETERANOS*, CHULILLA, SPAIN.
© *STU LITTLEFAIR*

In basic climbing terms, you should aim to do 10 to 30 hard moves and you can tailor this to the length of route or boulder problem that you're focusing on. Work on a 1:3 work:rest ratio, so if you're climbing for 1 minute, rest for 3 minutes between climbs. Aim for four or five bouts of climbing. You'll have to try really hard, and ideally you'll get the difficulty right so that you are falling off towards the end on your last couple of bouts.

A classic exercise for training anaerobic fitness on a bouldering wall is 4x4s. Pick four boulder problems at about 70 per cent of your max. Climb problem number one four times back to back. Rest for three times your climbing time and repeat the process with problems two, three and four.

Ideally do this on problems with about ten moves, and with a consistent level of difficulty throughout – nothing too cruxy. It's also a good idea to slightly vary the style of each of the four problems, so not just four overhanging crimp problems. Pick something steep and burly, something on slopers, something requiring good body tension, and so on.

Short endurance training is very intense. You'll definitely need a rest day afterwards, and maybe one before in order to ensure you're feeling rested and strong so you can perform so many hard moves.

To achieve gains in short endurance you'll need to train a couple of times a week for at least six weeks.

EXERCISE	Long Endurance Fingerboard Training
GOOD FOR	Trains recovery on a climb, or between attempts and between sessions
DESCRIPTION	6 x 7:3 repeaters on a comfy edge. Rest for 1 minute. This is one set.
SETS	Perform ten sets to give 10 minutes of hanging time. Rest for ten minutes. This is one bout.
BOUTS	Three bouts to give a total of 30 minutes of hanging time.
LOAD	Use a pulley to reduce the load to 30 to 40 per cent of your maximum hang on the edge you're training on. The aim is to spend a long time at a very low level of pump.
REST	Use a 1:1 work:rest ratio. So, rest for 1 minute between sets, and for 10 minutes between bouts.
PROGRESSION	Reduce the assistance to increase the load.
FREQUENCY	Two sessions a week.
HOW LONG FOR	At least 8 weeks and up to 16 weeks.
WHEN	This is a low-intensity exercise and so is easy to fit in around other training – try to do it after any other sort of climbing and never before any kind of strength training.

EXERCISE	Short Endurance Fingerboard Training
GOOD FOR	Training the ability to do more hard moves in a row without powering out
DESCRIPTION	6 x 7:3 repeaters on a comfy edge. Rest for 3 minutes. This is one set.
SETS	Perform six sets to give 6 minutes of hanging time. This is one bout.
BOUTS	One bout of this is enough as the intensity is very high.
LOAD	Use a pulley or added weight to adjust the load to 70 to 80 per cent of your maximum on the edge you're training on. You should be fighting really hard to hold on, and probably be failing on your final hangs of the last couple of sets.
REST	Use a 1:3 work:rest ratio. So, rest for 3 minutes between each set.
PROGRESSION	Increase the load by using less assistance or by adding weight.
FREQUENCY	Twice a week if short endurance is your training priority. Once a week if you're training strength alongside short endurance.
HOW LONG FOR	At least 6 weeks.
WHEN	Whenever you do this exercise, plan a rest day afterwards

ENDURANCE TRAINING ON THE FINGERBOARD

Long and short endurance can also be trained on the fingerboard – useful if you're unable to regularly access a climbing wall. This is incredibly boring, but it is effective: your forearms don't know the difference between fingerboarding and climbing but they will respond in the same way.

Long endurance fingerboard training

Throughout this aerobic endurance session you should feel a slight pump in your forearms. No more than 3/10 on the pump scale. You shouldn't be anywhere near failure – if you are, you should reduce the intensity. It may take you a bit of time to dial in the correct intensity – simply add or remove weight as necessary.

When training aerobic endurance, you are better off lowering the intensity and completing all the sets, rather than having the intensity too high and not getting to the end of your sets.

Short endurance fingerboard training

This is a hard exercise and you'll have to really bite down to get through all the sets. You'll need a rest day after this as it's pretty intense.

THE PEAK

The training methods recommended above will help you to build a good base of endurance. For your 'base phase' of training, try to do about two hours of long endurance and two sessions of short endurance per week for about eight weeks.

For optimal performance you should aim to supplement your base phase with a higher intensity peak phase of endurance training for six weeks before you want to be at your best. Peak phase training should be as specific to your goals as you can make it.

This might sound daunting and complex, but essentially it means that you should train on something as close in difficulty, length and style to your goal as you can. It might mean making up a circuit of the right length with similar crux moves. Or climbing some similar routes at the climbing wall on the correct angle or hold types. The more similar you can make your peak phase training to your goal, the more beneficial the training will be.

Summary

Long/aerobic endurance provides a low level of energy for a long time. Having a good level of aerobic fitness will help you to recover on a rest during a climb, between climbs and even between sessions. Training long endurance is easy, but it's boring.

Short/anaerobic endurance provides a high level of energy for a shorter and finite amount of time. A good level of short endurance will mean you can do more hard moves in a row without getting pumped or 'powering out'. Training short endurance is hard and painful, but it can be pretty satisfying.

After building a good endurance base, you can hone your endurance more specifically to your goals with six weeks of **peak phase** training.

FOOTLESS TRAINING

Previously, when thinking about training strength and power, the default approach was to head to the campus board. In the 1980s and 1990s this was a cutting-edge device, quite often literally – some edges that were climbed footless. At the time the campus board was a good idea, when most climbing walls were vertical brick walls, but these days the old-school campus board has more limitations than benefits. Modern climbing walls have developed so far and become so good that the campus board seems massively dated.

Limitations of campus boards:

/ The gaps between the rungs are very big: the step between pulling from one rung to the next is too large for steady, measured progress.

/ Generally, for strength and power training of the fingers, campus rungs are simply too big. How many really hard boulder problems can you think of that have a hold the size of a campus rung on them? OK, maybe a few, but they also involve much more than simply doing a fast one-armer on a fairly large hold. You'd usually have to get your body involved a lot as well.

/ Climbers tend to default to a half crimp or full open hand on the campus board as the rungs lend themselves to this type of grip. While this isn't necessarily a bad thing, it is rather limited.

/ The skin of the pinkie gets savaged by the repeated, grinding punishment off the same sized radius on the same hold.

/ Campus boards only work the pulling muscles in one plane – straight up and down. Little or no sideways movement is generated.

/ Doing big ladder moves such as 1–4–7 or

1–5–9 is fairly learned: you have to dial in the movement, and as you do it gets easier and easier – actual strength gains are minimal.

/ While on the face of it, campus boards are a standardised device, very few of them are the same. Expect to find different angles, different rungs and different rung spacings. Trying to replicate a session across a number of different campus boards is usually problematic.

Campus boards have their place for basic strength tests, strength endurance exercises and all-out endurance training performed with feet on, but a much better way of training footless climbing is to climb footless on a climbing wall or board.

Advantages of footless climbing on boards or boulder problems:

/ Hold style and size is varied: sometimes you'll have to pinch the holds, sometimes you'll be crimping them or open-handing them. The holds will also be at different angles, not just horizontal.

/ Move size and direction is varied: you can move sideways, up and down, do crossovers, come in close and so on. This means you will be able to effectively train your larger pulling muscles but also your smaller stabilising muscles through a large range of movement.

/ It's way more interesting and fun to train on a range of problem styles rather than just laddering away.

/ It is much easier to replicate a particular move or style of move and work on that.

/ It is much more applicable to real climbing if you're using a range of hold shapes and sizes and styles of move.

MY FOOTLESS BOARD EXPERIMENT. © *NED FEEHALLY*

FACILITIES

Generally, any climbing wall surface that's more than 20 degrees overhanging can be useful for footless climbing – unless it's covered in huge blobs or volumes which might get in the way. Horizontal roofs don't work so well as the holds usually have to be fairly large and you're not really pulling as most of your momentum is moving along the direction of the roof – you tend to dangle your way along.

If you're fortunate enough to have a decent board to train footless on, then brilliant. If you are even more fortunate and have the facilities or space available to build a specific footless board, then go for it. I built one a couple of years ago as an experiment. I love it!

Especially for short, efficient power sessions. Go for totally symmetrical with a range of hold shapes and sizes, all designed to work without feet – there is little point putting on a load of undercuts, for example.

Bear in mind, however, that climbing without your feet isn't going to do anything for your lower body. You also move very differently when you climb without your feet. Only ever training footless and then occasionally going climbing might not yield the best results on the rock. And if you're already good at footless climbing, then you're probably better off focusing your attention elsewhere ... slabs, perhaps.

When making up your own problems, focus on holds that are difficult to hold – not all jugs, and not all horizontal edges. This is great for developing good grip strength and the ability to generate momentum in different directions.

Tailor the problem length and style depending on the areas you feel you need to improve.

SPEED CAMPUSING

Pick a problem and climb it footless as fast as you can. You can also do this on a standard campus board. The idea is to maintain upwards momentum – or momentum in the direction of movement – at all times. When you hit a hold, pull on it *instantly*. Don't hang, readjust and get your body swinging in the right direction before pulling through to the next hold.

Speed campusing is a rudimentary form of plyometric training, which is designed to develop explosive power. Yet at the same time it is very applicable to climbing, which often relies on fast movements between handholds. Making up two-move campus problems to be climbed in this style is a great place to start. And as you develop speed you can add moves.

Hang a hold, blast upwards to the next hold and, as you hit it, start pulling through to the final hold. Once you can do it, keep trying it until you feel like you have the movement figured out and flowing nicely.

This exercise can be done with ladder-style problems (left, right, left and so on) or as double dynos (both hands moving at the same time).

FOOTLESS SESSIONS

As a general rule, if you can't do 10 pull-ups then I'd avoid doing any footless climbing as the intensity will be so much higher than you are used to. **Be careful.**

Pick a steep problem (more than 20 degrees overhanging to prevent your body from dragging up the wall) and climb it footless. Try to find problems with varied moves. For example, going out wide and coming in close, or big crossovers. Choose problems that challenge you in the ways that will benefit you the most. If you lack finger strength, you'll not get much out of campusing around on jugs.

Basically, try to spend as little time as possible on the intermediate hold. Over time you can stack these moves on top of each other.

DOUBLE DYNOS
These are quite advanced!

To train power and coordination, make up wild, footless double dynos, or a series of them in a row.

Try to focus on holds that aren't necessarily easy to hold. Leaping between jugs has its place, but it will be more beneficial to try to use the worst, most sloping holds you can.

You can also add a speed/plyometric element to double dynos. As soon as you catch some holds, instantly begin generating movement for the next holds. Basically, try to spend as little time as possible on the intermediate holds.

Remember
Footless climbing training is very intense on your upper body, and especially your fingers. It's also harsh on your skin as 100 per cent of your body weight is going through your fingers the whole time. I find that I need to limit the lengths of my footless sessions way more than normal board sessions. An hour of footless climbing is usually enough for me. I structure my footless sessions in a similar way to my normal board sessions: a circuit of warm-up problems followed by attempts at some projects in a couple of styles.

Summary

Footless climbing is great for getting stronger at holding on and pulling hard.

Old-school campus boards are quite limited; for a good footless session all you need is a slightly overhanging (minimum 20 degrees) bit of wall with some holds on it.

Footless climbing is great for getting the upper body working hard and helping you to get stronger, but remember that climbing involves so much more than just your fingers and arms. Don't only train footless and then wonder why you're not improving at climbing. Supplement your normal climbing with a few footless sessions when you need a strength top-up.

What can I do?

Pick existing climbs or make up your own and climb them footless. Focus on using holds that are hard to hold on to – don't just swing about on jugs.

Vary the style of the problems you are trying. Don't just do problems on tiny crimps or only do big moves.

TACTICS PART 3

Here's some advice about how to manage and maintain your skin. See pages 42 and 84 for more tactics.

REDUCING SWEAT
Keep the air moving around your hands. Use a fan or wave them in the air.

Keep your hands cool – don't put them in your pockets or hold a hot cup of tea for too long between climbs or attempts.

Go climbing when it's colder! It's usually more pleasant climbing in the sun, but it's not great for sweat-free conditions.

ANTIHYDRAL
The original skin-drying agent. This stuff is great. It dries your skin and toughens it. I find it a good option when climbing on sharp holds as it increases the toughness of my skin. I have used it while preparing to climb some gritstone projects which have very small, sharp holds on them, such as *Voyager Sit-Start* at Burbage.

However, the tough layer has a tendency to split or peel off after a few days, so I find that Antihydral is best used as a short-term solution to the problem of sweaty hands, and after a few uses I will lay off it for a while. It's also worth noting that it takes 12 to 24 hours to have its full effect, so furiously applying it while driving out to the crag is unlikely to yield any results, apart from a messy steering wheel.

When applying Antihydral, make sure it actually dries out on your skin. If it sits there on sweaty tips without drying, its potency is vastly reduced. I recommend applying it overnight.

Be very careful with getting Antihydral under your fingernails, or in/on existing splits or weak areas of skin. I have never had a problem with getting it in the seams of my fingers, but I know dry-handed folk who have had real problems with this. Splits in your seams are a nightmare to get rid of.

ALCOHOL
Alcohol is very useful for cleaning your hands before chalking up. It removes any grease and dirt that you might have on your skin, and it cools the skin. I carry a small bottle with me so I can clean my hands off before initially chalking up.

LIQUID CHALK
I don't tend to use alcohol-based liquid chalk very often. I prefer to keep my alcohol and chalk separate. However, on very dry days, or when climbing on wooden holds or smooth rock, a water-based liquid chalk can be a good way of adding a little moisture to your skin, enhancing grip.

RHINO SKIN SOLUTIONS
A game changer as far as I'm concerned. It has the same skin-drying effect as Anti-hydral, but without the toughening. For me it is perfect: It keeps my skin dry while also staying malleable and pretty split/tear proof.

I have naturally very sweaty fingers. Rhino Skin prolongs my sessions as having drier skin means I move a lot less on the holds and wear my skin down much more slowly as a result. A huge percentage of climbing at my limit comes down to skin and conditions. Rhino Skin seems to give me a bit of leeway as far as conditions are concerned. I find that I can climb in slightly higher temperatures or humidity without my skin instantly gushing sweat.

TRIM DANGLY BITS OF SKIN WITH A RAZOR BLADE.

As with Antihydral, I find that Rhino Skin needs 12 to 24 hours to take full effect. I see people spraying it on at the crag and whingeing that they are still sweating. Apply it overnight and leave it on to allow it time to do its job and clog those pesky sweat glands. I tend to use it a couple of times a week for a few weeks, and then I find that I don't need it for a few weeks. Rhino Skin makes a few products. Performance is their weakest skin drier, Dry is medium strength, and Tip Juice is the strongest. I use Tip Juice, but it's worth experimenting with the different options. As with Antihydral, try to avoid getting Rhino Skin under your fingernails or in any splits or weak bits of skin.

RHINO SKIN SOLUTIONS SPIT

Having recently discovered this, it's become a go-to product for training on wood or smooth holds indoors. It's designed for people with really dry skin, to add a bit of moisture so they can get more grip. Shauna has dry skin and uses loads of Spit whenever she is training, competing or rock climbing. Personally, I don't have dry skin, but I do like training on very smooth wooden holds. Spit gives me a bit of extra tackiness which makes a huge difference on wooden holds. With this I feel like I can train more consistently as skin variabilities seem to matter less. Worth a

try even if you don't have dry skin. Spit also works really well on smooth rock types, such as polished limestone, quartzy sandstone and polished granite, and in very dry climates. Spray it on, let it dry and then chalk up as normal. Repeat as many times as you need during a session.

SANDPAPER

It's good to keep your skin smooth as it can reduce the chance of splitting. Use sandpaper to (lightly) sand down rough areas between attempts on a climb. That said, I see people furiously sanding their hands between *every* go on a problem. This seems daft. Only sand away what is absolutely necessary as skin is a precious resource. I sometimes sand my skin after climbing when it's dry, or even when wet to remove any uneven bits that I notice. I use 120 grit sandpaper, and the cloth-backed stuff tends to last longer.

KNIFE/RAZOR BLADE

I use a knife or razor blade to trim off any dangly bits that might tear and bleed. Useful in situations where sanding won't quite work. And, again, only remove the bits that are likely to cause a problem. Be careful not to slip and end your climbing day!

ARM
EXERCISES

Having a strong upper body is useful for climbing, but it's not the be all and end all. Ultimately, it's our fingers that attach us to the rock, resin or wood. That said, being able to bend our arms is important and training our arms is easy and fairly satisfying.

Arm strength increases much faster than finger strength because it relies on big muscle groups which adapt rapidly to training stimuli.

You can dip in and out of arm training rather than doing it consistently and regularly – unlike finger strength training. If you feel like you need more pull, do eight to ten sessions on these sorts of exercises over five or six weeks and you'll see an improvement, but then take a break from them for a bit, or at least reduce the amount you do, because you only need so much strength in your arms and it's easy to overdo it and pick up an injury.

Tips

Strength training is all about quality so rest until you feel fully recovered.

Always train through the full range of motion, and lower slowly and in control. One rep is the full up and down movement, not just the up part.

You can easily alter the exercises by using a wider or narrower grip on a bar.

You can use two arms or one.

The first exercise works more of the strength endurance side, rather than outright strength.

ON THE MINUTES

A very simple exercise that can be done pretty much anywhere if you have something to hang from. Shauna does on the minutes as part of her warm-up for pretty much every session.

Choose an appropriate number of pull-ups based on your ability – it could be one or ten. Start the clock and perform the pull-ups. Rest for the remainder of the minute and repeat 'on the minute' – ten times in total. Over time you can increase the number of pull-ups per minute.

Add press-ups if you want to spice things up.

The following exercises are outright strength exercises so make sure you rest for at least 3 minutes between sets to ensure the quality of each set is as high as possible.

MAX PULL-UPS

Add or subtract an appropriate amount of weight using a harness/pulley (see page 58) or weight vest to find the sweet spot where one to three pull-ups is the absolute maximum you can do. One to three pull-ups in a row will target your maximum strength. Aim for a total of five sets at your maximum total load. Rest for 3 to 5 minutes between each set to keep the quality as high as you can.

PYRAMIDS

Pyramids are weighted pull-ups but with gradually increasing and then decreasing weight: as the weight increases, the number of reps decreases, and vice versa. Perform the sets as follows and rest for 3 minutes between each set.

/ **Set 1:** six pull-ups
/ **Set 2:** four pull-ups
/ **Set 3:** two pull-ups
/ **Set 4:** one pull-up
/ **Set 5:** two pull-ups
/ **Set 6:** four pull-ups
/ **Set 7:** six pull-ups

OFFSET PULL-UPS WITH WEIGHT TAKEN OFF WITH A PULLEY SET-UP.

OFFSET PULL-UPS

If you're not quite at the stage of being able to do one-armers these are a great way to load one arm more than the other. Use a pulley system, rope or resistance band for the lower arm to take off some of the load.

ONE-ARMERS

As above, you can remove weight with a pulley system or resistance band, or add weight if you're a hero!

OFFSET PULL-UPS WITH WEIGHT TAKEN OFF WITH A BAND.

NEGATIVES: STARTING POSITION.

NEGATIVES: LOWER SLOWLY.

NEGATIVES

Negative pull-ups are a great way to break through a plateau. Your muscles are always stronger when resisting a load (eccentric movement), rather than pulling against one (concentric movement). Therefore, you can work the muscles more by performing negatives.

Get a helping hand such as a spotter or a chair to stand on so you can start the exercise in a locked-off position. Now lower as slowly as possible.

Try to add or remove enough weight so that you can't lower much slower than 8 seconds.

Perform on both arms or just one, and do five sets with 3 minutes rest between each set.

Summary

When it comes to arm exercises, do a block of training but don't overdo it.

Focus on quality and make sure you're rested before training strength.

CORE

THE AUTHOR ON *MISS SCHWEIZ*, CHIRONICO, SWITZERLAND.
© *NICK BROWN*

What is 'core strength' or 'body tension'?

I would define body tension in climbing as our ability to maintain a solid frame, from our fingers to our toes, as we move between holds. It encompasses our ability to get our hands and feet where we need them, and to keep them in contact with the holds throughout a climbing movement.

I often hear it said that body tension is the ability to hold the swing when our feet cut loose. The problem with this is that it's easy to kill a swing and hold on if the handholds feel big; it's much harder when the handholds are bad. Therefore, the ability to kill a swing is mainly a function of finger strength, not 'body tension'. However, body tension is useful after we have stopped the swing for getting our feet back on to the wall – exactly where they need to be.

Our fingers are our body's upper attachment point. Our feet are its lower attachment point. If the handholds or footholds are positive or incut, we'll need to generate less tension between our hands and feet to keep our feet on the wall. As the handholds or footholds get worse, our body will have to take up the slack in order to make sure everything stays solid as we move.

Basically, on steep terrain, body tension is as much a function of finger strength as it is body strength. However, even with maximum finger strength, some climbers still find they have a floppy body on steep terrain. For many climbers, some supplementary strength exercises can help improve their body tension.

WHERE DOES BODY TENSION COME FROM?

The idea of body tension often causes confusion. 'Core' strength comes from so much more than just the 'core' muscles (the abdominals and lower back). It seems that some climbers think if they do a couple of sit-ups, they'll be able to keep their feet on while they climb or hold on when their feet cut loose.

Imagine climbing a steep wall with sloping footholds. If the handholds are jugs you will generally be able to keep your feet on. If the handholds are small or poor, you will find yourself jumping between handholds with your feet swinging about. Unless you are relatively new to climbing, or you avoid steep climbing like the plague, this is unlikely to be because your core is weak; rather it is because your fingers aren't strong enough to allow your body to work properly to keep your feet on.

Climbing-specific body tension comes from strength in the legs, glutes, lower back and shoulders as much as the abs. It also comes from the body's coordination – its ability to fire everything at the right time. You need to be relaxed and flowing when you climb, but also able to apply maximum force at exactly the point at which you need it. You don't want to be rigid while you climb, but you do want to be able to stiffen up for a split second while your hand moves from one hold to the next,

SHAUNA TRAINING TENSION WITH POOR FOOTHOLDS.

in order to maintain a solid position with your remaining points of contact.

Body tension is often as much about pushing with your body while pulling with your hands, as it is about clawing in with your feet. Having a rippling six-pack will only get you so far!

CLIMBING-BASED CORE EXERCISES

The best way to develop climbing-specific core strength is by climbing a lot on steep terrain.

Ideally, you'll be climbing on an angle steeper than 45 degrees so that it is an effort to keep your feet on the wall. The shallower the angle, the easier it is to get weight through the feet.

As you are training your ability to keep your feet on, don't just jump your feet off if it makes the moves easier. The objective is to keep your feet on as you climb.

Climbing on sloping footholds will train your ability to push through bad footholds and keep your feet on as you move. Climbing on positive footholds will train your ability to pull in and claw with your feet.

Either way, the idea is to maintain pressure through the foothold in order to keep your foot in contact with it. This active engagement of your body throughout the move is what you should focus on. **Don't just view a foothold as the starting line for the move: you should be using it at the beginning, middle and end of the move.**

WALKAROUNDS ON THE BOARD.

Ultimately, if you can climb steep terrain on really poor footholds then you'll be laughing when you get to a big positive foothold or to easier-angled terrain.

MAKE UP BODY TENSION TRAINING PROBLEMS

In an ideal world, you would make up problems on a board. However, you can use any steep climbing surface if you don't have access to a board. As with all climbing training methods, if you are actually climbing, you'll have more fun and will get more out of your session.

Make up moves that use poor footholds and try to keep the footholds far away from your hands – either low down or out to the sides. As soon as you bring your feet high, you can get more pressure through the footholds as

they are closer to you – this defeats the point of the exercise.

A good training system is to have a selection of standard problems that you can normally do, but try to climb them with poorer footholds, or with footholds in different positions. If you get into the habit of doing this as a part of your warm-up circuit, you'll be training this every session.

WALKAROUNDS

Pull on with a couple of good handholds (holding on should feel fairly easy) and walk your feet around a selection of poor footholds without them popping off. Try to extend as far away from the handholds as you can, both directly below you and out to the sides.

FEET OFF AND HANG ON EVERY MOVE.

NO CUT LOOSE

Climb a selection of easier problems while maintaining tension and keeping your feet on for every single move. You could even have an entire session on your board or at the climbing wall where this is your main focus. While it's often an unnatural way to climb and can actually make some moves on steep terrain a bit harder, it's great for working body tension and footwork.

FEET OFF AND HANG ON EVERY MOVE

Between each move, take your feet off, stop any swing, then put your feet back on and continue. Of course, this exercise is not about keeping your feet on, but it is good training

for getting your feet back on, and it slows the pace of your climbing, which on a board is often a useful thing to do. On boards we often climb unusually fast, but on rock or modern competition-style boulder problems we will tend to spend much more time hanging on and moving our feet or body around between each move.

BAR-BASED EXERCISES

While I think that floor-based 'core' exercises will do little to benefit your climbing, there are many ways of training core strength with front-lever-style exercises while hanging from a bar. These can be useful if you don't have easy access to a steep wall or you want to train some body tension while resting your fingers. Here are some ideas.

WINDSCREEN WIPERS STARTING POSITION.

WINDSCREEN WIPERS: ROTATE TO ONE SIDE AND THEN THE OTHER.

TUCK FRONT LEVER.

ONE-LEG FRONT LEVER.

FRONT LEVER.

WINDSCREEN WIPERS

Hang from the bar. Raise your back parallel with the ground and hinge your legs at the waist so they're at 90 degrees to your body – they'll be pointing upwards. Lower your legs to one side until they are parallel with the floor, then raise them back to the centre and lower to the other side. Continue alternating sides. Try to keep your legs straight. If you can't straighten them then you could probably do with stretching your hamstrings (see page 169).

TUCK FRONT LEVER

Hang from the bar. Tuck your knees into your chest and lift your legs and hips until your back is parallel with the floor, with your knees still tucked up. Keep your lower back straight, not curled upwards. Concentrate on pulling your shoulder blades back rather than hanging out of your shoulders.

To increase the difficulty, lift your legs so they are at 90 degrees to your back.

ONE-LEG FRONT LEVER

As for a tuck front lever, but straighten one leg (keeping it parallel with the ground) to increase the leverage and difficulty of the exercise. Alternate legs each time.

FRONT LEVER

This time, both legs will be straight. Hang from the bar with perfect form for as long as you can. Remember to keep your legs and back straight and parallel with the floor. You can make this exercise harder by adding ankle weights.

THRUST UP INTO FRONT LEVER

From hanging on the bar, thrust your body upwards into the front lever position and lower back down slowly – and in control.

Add ankle weights if it's all too easy. These exercises can also be done on handholds or some jugs on a fingerboard instead of a bar.

SHAUNA COXSEY ON *NEW BASE LINE*, MAGIC WOOD, SWITZERLAND. © *LUKA FONDA*

Summary

Core strength or body tension comes from your whole body, not just your abs! Learning exactly when you need to engage your core and when it can be relaxed is a huge part of climbing technique.

Body tension can be easily trained by climbing on steep surfaces and trying to keep your feet on as you move. The more sloping the footholds, the harder this becomes.

There are various exercises you can do to supplement your climbing-based body tension training.

What can I do?

Practise climbing on steep terrain with poor footholds and concentrate on keeping your feet on the wall, even if it would feel easier to take them off and jump between the holds.

Holding on to some good handholds on a steep wall and walking your feet around on poor footholds is great training for keeping your feet on.

Various front-lever-style exercises can be useful if you don't have easy access to a steep wall, or if you want to train your body tension while resting your fingers.

FLEXIBILITY & MOBILITY

THE AUTHOR FLASHING *TRUST ISSUES*, ROCKLANDS, SOUTH AFRICA.
© *SHAUNA COXSEY*

I find it strange and quite frustrating that some climbers are so inflexible. They are happy to spend hours hanging from a fingerboard or swinging about on a board, yet seem reluctant to devote just a bit of time to improving their flexibility and mobility. Being flexible and mobile is absolutely essential for climbing well. All climbers can benefit from doing stretching or mobility work.

FLEXIBILITY VS MOBILITY

Flexibility is the ability to bend our body into a shape. Mobility is the ability to bend it into a shape *under the control of our own muscles* – in our case, *while we are climbing*. For example, you might be able to bring your knee to your chest by using your hands (flexibility), but how high can you lift your knee without the assistance from your hands (mobility)?

While flexibility on its own is advantageous for climbing, we also need the strength to use it – this provides us with mobility.

Flexibility + Strength = Mobility

We can never be too bendy for climbing, certainly in terms of our lower body. As long as our upper body is fairly solid, it is also advantageous to have some mobility up there too. This helps us to avoid injuries as our body can move between positions more easily, and move into a larger range of positions.

STRETCHING

Stretching is the classic method of improving flexibility. Hold a position for a long time, and with repeated attempts the position will become easier to achieve.

These days there are also all sorts of mobility exercises which we can do, where we move a joint – or a few at once – through a range of movement with some resistance. This style of mobility training is very useful for targeting weak areas as it trains some strength into the system as well as increasing our range of motion.

© BAND OF BIRDS

I prefer good old-fashioned stretching. I find it quite relaxing and it is something I can do anywhere, with zero equipment or set-up. I have stretched every day for the last 20 years.

> Rather than stretching, Shauna prefers to do a range of mobility exercises a couple of times a week. But she also does a lot of flexibility work on the climbing wall while she warms up for every climbing session – high-stepping, bridging and holding odd positions for extended time periods as she moves around the wall.

Don't worry about becoming flexible but not having the strength to use it. As your range of motion increases you can adjust your climbing accordingly, thereby using your new range and building strength within it. You'll gain flexibility slowly, so you should easily be able to adjust your climbing to any flexibility improvements that you have made.

This is unless, of course, you stretch and become very bendy but continue to climb totally front on and in a basic way, and never learn to reap the rewards of having the bendy body which you worked so hard to get. I can

MICKY PAGE ON *BLACK EAGLE*, ROCKLANDS, SOUTH AFRICA.
© *NICK BROWN*

think of more than one example of this. The climber who is on paper very flexible but isn't able to use it as they climb. If you don't apply your flexibility to your climbing, you'll not learn to use it or develop the strength that you need to use it, ultimately limiting your mobility.

It is easy to avoid stretching or put it on the back burner in favour of strength training. However, the advantages of being flexible are pretty much endless. Watch a video of Adam Ondra climbing. He's obviously incredibly strong and fit, but what really jumps out is the way he moves. He's very, very bendy, and snakes his way up the rock, often with huge drop knees, heel hook rockovers or obscene frog manoeuvres.

These days you won't come across a very good, well-rounded climber who isn't relatively bendy.

No excuses.

ADVANTAGES OF STRETCHING

Increasing your flexibility will help you climb better as you'll more easily be able to place your feet where you need them and be able to put more weight through them once they are there.

Increasing your flexibility will make certain moves that once felt very difficult, feel almost trivial – such as a high step on a climb you've always wanted to do.

It's very easy to see improvements in flexibility, and just 10 minutes every day is easy to fit in and can be enough. More is better, but consistency is key. I recommend getting into the habit of stretching regularly. Build it into your morning or night-time routine, your warm-up before or cool down after a session, or during rest periods when fingerboarding.

Unlike strength training, your muscles need very little recovery after stretching. So, you can stretch more or less as much as you want to or have time to and see benefits.

Greater mobility can help to minimise the risk of injury. Climbing these days involves all sorts of lower body contortion – knee bars, heel hooks, toe hooks and so on – and without a decent level of mobility in your lower body you'll be putting your joints at risk.

DISADVANTAGES OF STRETCHING

None really, apart from the time it takes to do it – you'll have less time to show off doing one-armers in front of people!

SHOULD I STRETCH BEFORE I CLIMB?

Some studies suggest that holding static stretches before exercising can temporarily reduce the amount of power your muscles can output. Realistically, though, this won't affect you negatively unless you decide to spend ages stretching out your forearm muscles right before you pull on (since your forearm muscles are generally the only

muscle group that will be working at 100 per cent when you're climbing).

If a specific move requires you to stretch a particular muscle group in order to get into a position more easily, then go for it. But generally, I find dynamic stretches and warm-up exercises more useful as a climbing warm-up than static stretches.

Just make sure you take it easy. 1990s-style flailing arm windmills aren't recommended for your poor shoulders!

FORM A HABIT

As you see improvements in your flexibility you should recognise this and start to climb in a way which takes advantage of it. This will help you to climb better and will also provide you with a bit of extra motivation so you continue stretching.

Substituting a small percentage of your climbing or training time for some stretching is possibly one of the most useful things you can do to benefit your climbing.

Try to form a stretching habit. It could be 10 minutes every morning, 15 minutes at the end of every session, 20 minutes every evening while watching TV, or a single one-hour session each week. It's up to you, but little and often is more useful than a lot followed by nothing at all.

1 FLEXORS STRETCH.

2 EXTENSORS STRETCH.

RECOMMENDED STRETCHES

As we've seen above, stretching is really important and most of us will benefit from doing more of it – and for the vast majority of climbers, simply doing any stretching would be a good start. But it's not just about being bendy. When we climb, we need to be able to pull or push out of lots of positions. Ideally, we will be bendy, strong and mobile.

Here are my 10 favourite stretches and mobility exercises. These exercises have been part of my everyday routine for many years.

I hold stretches for at least 30 seconds, or 10 slow breaths. But you can hold them for a few minutes at a time. I repeat each stretch at least three times. Don't force them too hard. Slow and steady wins the race. Stretching should feel mildly uncomfortable, but not painful.

UPPER BODY
FOREARM STRETCHES

Most of us have pretty beaten-up forearm muscles as we rely so much on them when we climb. Stretching both sets of forearm muscles, flexors and extensors, will help you to keep your elbows, wrists and fingers feeling much more healthy, and will reduce the risk of injury.

1   **Flexors stretch:** Flatten your hands on to a flat surface with your fingers pointing back towards you, straighten your elbows and gently lean backwards.

2   **Extensors stretch:** Curl your fingers up and back, straighten your elbow and stretch out using your other hand for support. Swap sides and repeat.

3 CAT-COW STRETCH: UPPER POSITION.

3 CAT-COW STRETCH: LOWER POSITION.

4 SUPINE SPINAL TWIST.

5 ROADKILL STRETCH.

BACK STRETCHES

A lot of climbers develop a fairly stiff back. A combination of not a lot of stretching and piling on a fair bit of muscle is a recipe for a lack of mobility. Also, people who work at a desk, or spend large parts of the day stationary, can develop stiffness in the back. The spine is supposed to be able to bend and move, and keeping it mobile will help your whole upper body to work more efficiently.

It's useful to breathe very deeply during all of these stretches. The expansion of your ribs and chest will help to stretch a lot of the muscles around your torso, hopefully allowing all the joints to move more easily.

3 **Cat–cow stretch:** This stretch/exercise should help to get your spine moving as it was always meant to. It's performed kneeling on all fours: hold at the top and bottom positions for a couple of seconds. Repeat five times up and five times down.

4 **Supine spinal twist:** Lie down on your back with your arms out straight to the sides for balance. Keeping one leg straight, lift the other leg to 90 degrees and let it flop across your body. Hold this position for 10 deep breaths and then repeat on the other side.

5 **Roadkill stretch:** Another good stretch for back mobility. Lie down on your front with your arms out straight to the sides for balance. Now raise your left leg and flop it over the top of your right leg, aiming to reach your right hand with your foot. Hold for 10 deep breaths and alternate sides.

LOWER BODY

6 Squat: I am constantly surprised at how many climbers simply can't squat down! Squats are great and they stretch the glutes, calves, quads and hips. With your heels on the ground and keeping a straight back with your shoulders and head up, squat down as low as you can (while maintaining form) and hold this position.

For an added hip stretch, push outwards on your knees with your elbows.

6 SQUAT.

7 Hamstrings stretch: Flexible hamstrings are essential for heel hooking, but also for getting the feet high and into weird positions. Simply bend down and touch your toes. Keep your heels on the floor and your knees straight and reach down as far as you can and hold this position.

8 High steps: Climbing generally involves stepping the feet up on to footholds, and then standing up on them. The higher you can step your feet, the easier things will feel. Also, the easier it is for you to lift your feet into these high positions, the less you'll have to lean out from the wall in order to do it, reducing the likelihood of you falling off. Step your foot up on to a chair, table or out in front of you on the floor and lean into the stretch.

7 HAMSTRINGS STRETCH.

9 Calf stretch: Sloping footholds, especially on lower-angled terrain, require good ankle flexibility. The lower you can drop your heels, the more foot surface area you'll be able to get on to the footholds. This type of move has become a mainstay of modern competition climbing – trying to get as much surface area of the foot on to a volume as possible. Toe hooks also

8 HIGH STEPS.

10 FROG POSE HIP STRETCH.

10 PROGRESSION: BOX SPLITS.

9 CALF STRETCH.

require you to be able to pull backwards with your toes, and tightness in your calves will limit your ability to do this.

Simply drop your ankles off a step, either both together or one at a time, or stick your toes up against a wall and lean into it.

10 Frog pose hip stretch: Getting your weight in close to the wall requires you to be able to open your hips and turn your knees out. Flexible hips are essential for efficient climbing.

Lie on the floor and spread your knees out as far as you can. If you find these easy, you can progress to box splits.

Summary

Being flexible and mobile is absolutely essential for climbing well. All climbers can benefit from doing stretching or mobility work.

Having more mobility will allow you to move your body more efficiently as you climb, making it all feel much easier. Stretching can also help to keep your body in better condition, minimising the risk of injury.

What can I do?

Form a regular stretching habit. You'll quickly notice the benefits as you climb and it will encourage you to stick with it.

THE AUTHOR ON *BIG GOLDEN*, CUVIER REMPART, FONTAINEBLEAU, FRANCE. © *NICK BROWN*

HAND &
UPPER BODY
MAINTENANCE

As climbers we put our bodies through a whole lot of abuse. We pull as hard as we possibly can on small holds, often in the cold and usually without much in the way of a warm-up.

We could all do with putting a bit more effort into a few maintenance exercises which help to keep our bodies healthy, injury free and functioning as well as they possibly can. I know it sounds sensible and not much fun, but having a healthy body that allows us to go climbing as much as we want is surely something we should all strive for.

There is an almost infinite number of exercises and stretches we can do, but I have narrowed it down to a few simple things which we can use as a part of our warm-up, on rest days or even while at working at a desk.

HANDS

We can all benefit from taking more care of our hands. Few climbers consider doing anything other than pulling really hard and then potentially doing the odd stretch or cooling their fingers around a pint glass. Our hands are our main contact with the wall, and we ask an awful lot of them. So we should make time for some TLC for strength, health and injury prevention.

LUMBRICAL STRENGTHENING
The lumbricals help to move and hold our fingers in positions that are useful for crimping. Weakness in the lumbricals can lead to unstable fingers when we crimp, and can cause pain in the hands. If you press between the metacarpals in your palm, you may feel tender areas. It's likely that these are your lumbricals.

It's good to get into the habit of massaging them, and it's also good to train some strength into them. Try the following two exercises.

Ball squeezes
Get a foam ball and squeeze it between straight fingers and thumb, either with all four fingers at once, or with individual fingers. Keep your fingers straight! To begin with, go for higher reps (15 to 20) to get the muscles going, but over time you can increase the intensity with a tougher ball and perform fewer reps.

Finger slides
Place your hands flat on a table, palms down. Keep your wrists in contact with the table and press your fingertips down with straight fingers. Now slowly slide your fingertips towards your wrists as far as you can go – while keeping straight fingers and wrists in contact with the table. Then lift up your fingers and return them to the starting position. Again, start with 15 to 20 lower-intensity reps but build up to doing fewer reps at a higher intensity. You can adjust the intensity by simply pressing down harder with your fingertips. It shouldn't hurt, but you should be able to feel the muscles begin to get tired.

BALL SQUEEZES.

INTEROSSEI STRENGTHENING.

INTEROSSEI STRENGTHENING

The interossei adduct and abduct the fingers – think Mr Spock doing the Vulcan salute – and stabilise them as we hold on, especially in a crimp position. It's worth training them as weaknesses can cause knuckle pain. Use a squashy ball and simply squeeze it between your fingers with a scissor action. Keep your fingers straight and work your way along the fingers.

FINGER SLIDES: STARTING POSITION.

Begin with higher reps (15 to 20) and as you notice some gains in strength you can increase the resistance with a stiffer ball and reduce the number of reps.

FINGER SLIDES: FINISHING POSITION.

TENDON GLIDES SEQUENCE.

OLD CLIMBER HANDS! © *MATT BIRD*

WRISTS & ELBOWS

Climbers have well-developed finger and wrist flexor muscles, but most climbers do little to help keep their finger and wrist extensors healthy. An imbalance between these flexors and extensors can lead to wrist pain, elbow pain or simply pain in the extensors as they are trying too hard to keep up with the flexors. I suffered from pain in my extensors and elbows for years until I eventually worked out that they were simply too weak. A bit of training with the following exercises sorted me out and I haven't had a problem with them since.

TENDON GLIDES
Many climbers struggle to even move their fingers through their full range of motion!

Keeping your fingers moving and fully mobile is essential for keeping them healthy. It's worth trying to get into the habit of simply moving your fingers through their full range, from straight to fully curled up while keeping the fingertips in contact with your palm. It's not really a case of reps and sets, but instead adding this exercise into your daily routine. I do loads of this, especially on rest days when my fingers feel stiff or worked from a session.

FOREARM EXTENSOR CURLS
Hold a dumb-bell palm down, with your elbow at 90 degrees. Curl it upwards by flexing your wrist back, and then lower it back down to a neutral position – **not** below the level of the forearm. Support your forearm to ensure that you're only working the extensor muscles. You should perform low reps with heavy weights, rather than high reps, as you want to train the extensors' maximal strength. Five to ten reps, and three to five sets, is great.

FOREARM EXTENSOR HOLDS
As above, but simply hold the weight statically with a straight wrist. Aim to hold for a max-imum of 10 seconds for five sets per arm.

FOREARM EXTENSOR CURLS: STARTING POSITION.

FOREARM EXTENSOR CURLS: UPPER POSITION.

SHAUNA COXSEY ON *PENDRAGON*, ROCKLANDS, SOUTH AFRICA. © *NED FEEHALLY*

HANGING SHRUGS: STARTING POSITION.

HANGING SHRUGS: FINISHING POSITION.

PRESS-UP SHRUGS: STARTING POSITION.

PRESS-UP SHRUGS: FINISHING POSITION.

BACK: MODIFIED COBRA POSE.

BACK: MODIFIED COBRA POSE.

SHOULDERS

A lot has been written over the years about strengthening and maintaining the rotator cuff muscles. There are the classic TRX and ring exercises, such as I, Y and T, which are definitely worth investigating if you're unfamiliar with them.

However, what's not talked about so much is mobility and strength in the shoulder blades – the scapulae. The idea isn't to fix them in position as you train and climb, but to allow them to move! The shoulder blades need to be able to move through their full range of motion, and be strong throughout their full range. The following two exercises are great added to your warm-up to get your shoulders moving well.

HANGING SHRUGS
Dangle from a bar and sink as far down as you can, allowing your shoulder blades to move. Now, while maintaining straight arms and a straight back throughout the exercise, slowly pull (shrug) up with just your shoulder blades – imagine trying to pinch them together at the top of the movement. Now lower, slowly, all the way back down – as low as you can go.

Work up to holding the top and bottom positions for 5 seconds, and repeat the exercise five times. It might feel like you're not doing much, but remember the aim of this exercise is to increase mobility as much as to develop strength, so stick with it.

PRESS-UP SHRUGS
From a press-up position, with your arms, legs and back straight, sink slowly downwards

with your shoulders, keeping your arms straight – imagine that you're pinching something between your shoulder blades. Now press (shrug) back up slowly, as high as you can, and repeat. Try to keep your neck straight, and your shoulders away from your ears.

Work up to holding the upper and lower positions for 5 seconds. You can start off in a kneeling press-up position to get used to the movement and then work up to doing it in a full press-up position.

BACK

While lower back mobility is important for climbers, mobility in the mid back (thoracic spine) is often overlooked. The mobility of the thoracic spine is crucial for allowing the shoulders to move properly, especially when we are reaching overhead. If you lift your arms above your head, that last 10 to 15 degrees of movement actually comes from your mid back.

This modified cobra pose will stretch your serratus anterior muscles which attach your ribs to your shoulder blades. Many climbers have tightness here which really limits the mobility of the mid back.

Lift one leg to 90 degrees and rotate your head and shoulders towards this leg. You should feel the stretch down the other side of your body. Hold the stretch for five deep breaths – the motion of breathing in will expand your rib cage and help the stretch work its magic. Repeat five times on each side.

QUICK
SESSIONS

FINGERBOARD

Here are some quick session ideas to help you get motivated. Make sure that you're warmed up and ready to go – don't just pile straight in!

To get the level correct for you, adjust the resistance by adding or removing weight, or adjusting the hold size or grip position.

Concentrate on the form of your fingers. Maintain the exact grip position that you're aiming to train. Failure is the point when you lose form, rather than when you explode off the fingerboard.

REPEATERS
/ Pick a grip type.
/ Hang for 7 seconds and rest for 3 seconds and repeat six times to complete one set in 1 minute.
/ Rest for 3 to 5 minutes between sets and aim for three sets per grip type.

SHORT MAX HANGS
/ Pick a grip type.
/ Hang for roughly 10 seconds.
/ Rest for 2 to 3 minutes.
/ Perform three to five hangs with 2 to 3 minutes of rest between each hang to complete one set.

LONG MAX HANGS
/ Pick a grip type.
/ Hang for roughly 20 seconds.
/ Rest for 3 to 5 minutes.
/ Perform three to five hangs with 3 to 5 minutes of rest between each hang to complete one set.
/ You'll probably feel more fatigued after these than after short hangs, so be careful to rest appropriately afterwards.

TENDON HANGS
/ Pick a grip type.
/ Hang for roughly 45 seconds – you should reach failure at about this time.
/ Rest for five minutes.
/ Perform four hangs with 5 minutes of rest between hangs to complete one set.

ARMS
ON THE MINUTES
/ A very simple exercise to get the arms going.
/ Choose an appropriate number of pull-ups for your level and start a stopwatch.
/ Complete that number of pull-ups and rest for the remainder of the first minute.
/ Repeat on the minute, ten times.
/ Add press-ups if you're feeling spritely – either afterwards, or in the same minute!

NEGATIVES
/ Use one or two arms.
/ Pull up using assistance such as a chair (or your other arm if only using one arm) and lower down as slowly as possible and in control.
/ Adjust the load so it takes between 3 and 5 seconds to lower down.
/ Rest for 3 minutes between each set.
/ Complete five sets.

WEIGHTED PULL-UPS
/ Simple: add weight and do pull-ups!
/ Keep the load high and the reps low (a maximum of five pull-ups).
/ Compete five sets, with at least 3 minutes rest between each set.
/ Always lower down slowly and in control: no jumping off after doing the last pull-up without lowering down!

DON'T FORGET TO STRETCH!

BOARD

STRENGTH 1
/ Complete a five- to ten-problem warm-up circuit.
/ Now pick three projects at your limit and spend at least 15 minutes working each problem and trying to link the moves. Vary the style of each problem: one could be on small holds, one on pinches and one with big moves.
/ If you manage a problem, make up a new, harder problem and work on that.

STRENGTH 2
/ Complete a five- to ten-problem warm-up circuit.
/ Pick five problems at 75 to 95 per cent of your maximum. Add ankle weights and try to climb all five problems.

MILEAGE
/ Climb ten to fifteen problems at up to 75 per cent of your maximum. Rest for 2 to 5 minutes between each problem (depending on the problem length). Concentrate on climbing the problems well. Try to keep your feet on (when appropriate), rather than simply leaping between the holds.

SHORT ENDURANCE: 4X4s
/ Pick four boulder problems at about 70 per cent of your maximum. Don't pick cruxy problems; aim for sustained difficulty.
/ Climb four laps on problem number one back to back and rest for three times your climbing time.
/ Repeat on problem number two and continue for all four problems.
/ After a 15-minute rest you can do it all again if you want!

MAINTENANCE

FOREARM EXTENSOR CURLS

/ Hold a dumb-bell palm down in a neutral
position with your forearm supported.
/ Curl the weight upwards and back down
to the neutral position.
/ Aim to do sets of five to ten curls with
3 minutes of rest between each set.

LUMBRICAL FINGER SLIDES

/ Place your hands flat on a table.
/ Keeping your wrists in contact with the
table, press down with your fingertips
with straight fingers.
/ Now draw your fingertips slowly towards
your wrists as far as you can without lifting
your wrists.
/ Aim to do sets of five to ten slides and
adjust the intensity by pressing harder
with your fingertips.

STRETCHING

Because there are so many different stretches
that would benefit climbers and because I've
already narrowed these down in chapter 15
to what I consider are the most important, it
seems daft to shortlist the shortlist. Basically,
get on with it! Pick a couple and tag them on
to the end of your quick session and get into
the habit of doing this. Or do them when you're
having a morning coffee break, and so on.

You can do as much or as little as you can fit
into the time you have spare. Five minutes
here and there is better than nothing at all!
As I type this, I have my foot up on the desk
to stretch out my glute.

Hold each stretch for at least 30 seconds.
Ideally longer. Repeat as many times as you
can face!

Try to form a habit of stretching regularly.

QUICK SESSIONS: FINGERBOARD EXERCISE REFERENCE TABLES

FINGERBOARD EXERCISES: STRENGTH

EXERCISE	Repeaters
GOOD FOR	Strength/strength endurance
DESCRIPTION	Hang for 7 seconds, rest for 3 seconds. This is one rep. Six reps = one set and takes 1 minute.
SETS	One or two sets per grip type. Up to three grip types per session is enough.
REST	5 minutes between sets.
PROGRESSION	More/less hang time/rest per set, e.g. hang for 6 seconds, rest for 4 seconds. Add weight. Add sets per grip type. Use smaller holds.
HOW LONG FOR	I think you should always be training finger strength to some degree. Cycle between finger training methods throughout the year to keep your body on its toes. Repeaters are relatively safe as they're low impact.
WHEN	Always train strength when you're well rested and fresh.

EXERCISE	Short Max Hangs
GOOD FOR	Strength: neuromuscular gains
DESCRIPTION	Hang for 5 to 12 seconds. This is one rep. Three to five reps = one set.
SETS	One set can be enough, or repeat for up to five grip types.
LOAD	Adjust the load so 5 to 12 seconds is the absolute maximum you can achieve.
REST	2 to 3 minutes between each hang, or as long as you need so you can give 100 per cent effort again.
PROGRESSION	Add weight. Use smaller holds. One arm instead of two.
HOW LONG FOR	I think you should always be training finger strength to some degree. Cycle between finger training methods throughout the year to keep your body on its toes.
WHEN	Always train strength when you're well rested and fresh.

EXERCISE	Long Max Hangs
GOOD FOR	Strength: muscle size and longer-lasting gains
DESCRIPTION	Hang for 20 seconds. This is one rep. Three to five reps = one set.
SETS	One set can be enough, or repeat for up to five grip types.
LOAD	Adjust the load so 20 seconds is the absolute maximum you can achieve.
REST	3 to 5 minutes between hangs, or as long as you need so you can give 100 per cent effort again.
PROGRESSION	Add weight. More hangs per grip type. Use smaller holds. One arm instead of two.
HOW LONG FOR	I think you should always be training finger strength to some degree. Cycle between finger training methods throughout the year to keep your body on its toes.
WHEN	Always train strength when you're well rested and fresh.

EXERCISE	Tendon Hangs
GOOD FOR	Contact strength and tendon health
DESCRIPTION	Hang for 30 to 45 seconds. This is one rep. Three reps = one set.
SETS	One set per grip type; up to three sets in total.
LOAD	Adjust the load so you fail at about 45 seconds.
REST	5 minutes between hangs.
PROGRESSION	Add weight. Use smaller holds.
HOW LONG FOR	I think you should always be training finger strength to some degree. Cycle between finger training methods throughout the year to keep your body on its toes.
WHEN	Always train strength when you're well rested and fresh.

FINGERBOARD EXERCISES: ENDURANCE

EXERCISE	Long Endurance Fingerboard Training
GOOD FOR	Trains recovery on a climb, or between attempts and between sessions
DESCRIPTION	6 x 7:3 repeaters on a comfy edge. Rest for 1 minute. This is one set.
SETS	Perform ten sets to give 10 minutes of hanging time. Rest for ten minutes. This is one bout.
BOUTS	Three bouts to give a total of 30 minutes of hanging time.
LOAD	Use a pulley to reduce the load to 30 to 40 per cent of your maximum hang on the edge you're training on. The aim is to spend a long time at a very low level of pump.
REST	Use a 1:1 work:rest ratio. So, rest for 1 minute between sets, and for 10 minutes between bouts.
PROGRESSION	Reduce the assistance to increase the load.
FREQUENCY	Two sessions a week.
HOW LONG FOR	At least 8 weeks and up to 16 weeks.
WHEN	This is a low-intensity exercise and so is easy to fit in around other training – try to do it after any other sort of climbing and never before any kind of strength training.

EXERCISE	Short Endurance Fingerboard Training
GOOD FOR	Training the ability to do more hard moves in a row without powering out
DESCRIPTION	6 x 7:3 repeaters on a comfy edge. Rest for 3 minutes. This is one set.
SETS	Perform six sets to give 6 minutes of hanging time. This is one bout.
BOUTS	One bout of this is enough as the intensity is very high.
LOAD	Use a pulley or added weight to adjust the load to 70 to 80 per cent of your maximum on the edge you're training on. You should be fighting really hard to hold on, and probably be failing on your final hangs of the last couple of sets.
REST	Use a 1:3 work:rest ratio. So, rest for 3 minutes between each set.
PROGRESSION	Increase the load by using less assistance or by adding weight.
FREQUENCY	Twice a week if short endurance is your training priority. Once a week if you're training strength alongside short endurance.
HOW LONG FOR	At least 6 weeks.
WHEN	Whenever you do this exercise, plan a rest day afterwards

THE AUTHOR AT THE CLIMBING HANGAR MATCHWORKS IN LIVERPOOL.

PRO TIPS

ALEX PUCCIO

Alex is one of the strongest climbers on the planet, with some of the best pinch strength I have ever witnessed. She has won 14 bouldering world cup medals and climbed multiple Font 8b+ boulder problems. Since shifting her focus entirely to rock climbing, she has been racking up a huge tick list of hard, powerful boulder problems around the world, including *New Base Line* in Magic Wood, and *Jade* in Rocky Mountain National Park.

What is your 5-second maximum one-arm hang on the Beastmaker 2000 middle edge? (How much weight can you add and hang for 5 seconds?)

I have not really trained this at all, but have tried it a few times. The last time I tried it I weighed 57.6 kilograms and I was in the UK. Robin [O'Leary] wanted to see what I could hold, so he kind of tested me, but I didn't really rest much at all between different weight tests and it was at the end of a session. He had me start with something like 5 kilograms and he just kept jumping up in weight. I hung with 27 kilograms pretty easily for just over 5 seconds and so he had me try 29 kilograms and I hung for somewhere about 4 seconds. I haven't tried it since!

How long can you hold the Beastmaker six-millimetre micros for (two arms!)?

I have actually never tried to hang them or any of the sizes as long as I can, but instead I do sets of pull-ups on them or do a repeaters workout on them. For the pull-ups, I normally do something like five to eight pull-ups on the six-millimetres and then rest and do it again three or four times.

What is your maximum number of one-armers?

Six on a jug, two on the 10-millimetre edge. And my best clean one-arm pull-up with weight added is with +11 kilograms.

What is your favourite finger strength exercise?

Honestly, I have never really done a finger strength phase. When I get fitter and stronger and climb on rock A LOT, I normally can test everything and see I have massive gains. Maybe not quite the answer you are looking for, but for me, climbing all the time on rock makes my fingers the strongest.

What is the most common mistake people make when training?

Since coaching a lot of people at all different ability levels, I've noticed that people want to get strong or better too quickly, and they don't realise you actually have to be patient with all of it. Also, a HUGE thing is that lots of climbers actually avoid their weaknesses. I see lots of people who don't like to get on the 'easier' grades that feel hard for them, but they'd rather get on the 'harder'-graded climbs they can do. You won't become a well-rounded climber this way!

What is your advice for climbers who want to improve?

The hardest part is always starting! When starting a new training plan with exercises that you don't necessarily like or want to do, for me it's cardio, you just have to start doing it. Once you have started and got the ball rolling and into a routine you will feel very different about it all and get more and more

ALEX PUCCIO ON *SLASHFACE*, HUECO TANKS, USA. © *JOEL ZERR*

ADAM ONDRA AT THE 2019 IFSC CLIMBING WORLD CUP
IN MEIRINGEN, SWITZERLAND. © *RYU VOELKEL*

psyched for your training and your goals will become closer and closer! It's not a sprint, it's more like a lifelong marathon. You will always keep learning and want to improve different aspects of your climbing. Once you have reached one goal then you will quickly set another one and strive to reach that one!

Also, take your ego out of it if you want to improve! I always say, 'Hang up your ego at the front door when you come in to train, you can pick it up when you leave. There is no room for it in here if you want to improve!'

ADAM ONDRA

I don't really need to introduce Adam Ondra. He's the best climber who has ever lived. He's redpointed the hardest sport climbs in the world, climbed a load of the hardest boulder problems (flashing some of them!), won more world cup medals than I can list and made a quick ascent of the Dawn Wall, the hardest big wall in the world. Adam absolutely loves everything about climbing and leaves no stone unturned when it comes to training and preparation for his goals. Everybody should be more like Adam!

What is your maximum number of one-armers?

I once did 16 dynamic one-armers on the pull-up bar (taped one). Static, I can barely do one.

What is your favourite finger strength exercise?

For me, it would just be old-school crimpy bouldering on the spray wall with a strong crew, like Martin Stráník or Rishat Khaibullin (who is bloody strong at crimping). Otherwise, that one-centimetre slopey Beastmaker campus rung is just amazing. You can't crimp if you make longer moves – the edge is rounded enough to make it impossible to just 'hang' on your skin, so you really have to use finger strength to hold on.

What is the most common mistake people make when training?

When it comes to campusing or finger-boarding, I believe that if people want to train power, their rests are not long enough. And they end up working on more short power endurance. Pure power training is actually really boring: you should not feel tired, the exercise should be short and with at least 3 minutes' rest. For sure, the campus board

You have to work on your weaknesses to get better, so I call it the 70/30 rule: when training, work on your weaknesses 70 per cent of the time and your strengths 30 per cent of the time if you want to improve faster.

or fingerboard can be a tool for training power endurance (and I use it this way), but most people think of it and use it mainly for increasing their power.

Then, I believe the importance of climbing itself is often underestimated. Being strong helps, but being a good climber is better, and being a good and strong climber is the ultimate goal. But it is better to start with being a good climber, and only later focus on getting stronger. On the top of this, you can get strong just by climbing too. Campus boards and fingerboards are great and efficient tools, but they are more of in addition to training, not the core.

What is your advice for climbers who want to improve?

It depends a lot on what you want to focus on. Obviously, if you want to improve in outdoor sport climbing, training massive triple dynos will not help you very much. I would start with something that should be useful for everyone – competition boulderer or outdoor boulderer, or sport climber, indoors or outdoors. And that is training by bouldering on a spray wall. It is the most natural way to get stronger while still working on your technique.

The power you need to make hard moves on a spray wall is essential for sport climbers as the more confident you are on harder moves, the less you will get pumped. Power is essential for competition bouldering – even in those triple dynos it helps to be able to hold on small stuff – and sometimes, they set even hard old-school boulder problems. And for outdoor bouldering, it is pretty obvious.

Most importantly, you just have to love it. Don't do it for the goal, do it because you absolutely adore climbing and training. Enjoy the process and the success will come.

JERRY MOFFATT

Throughout the 1980s and 1990s, Jerry Moffatt was one of the best climbers in the world. The first climber to really embrace training, initially outdoors on the limestone crags in the Peak District, and then indoors in some of the first ever purpose-built training facilities. Jerry built the first board in his cellar in the mid 1980s. Soon after that he opened the world-famous Foundry climbing wall in Sheffield. He has made some of the most iconic first ascents in the world, including *The Ace* (Font 8b), *Dominator* (Font 8b) and *Liquid Ambar* (F8c+).

What is your maximum number of one-armers?

I could never do many one armers, probably two. I could do a one armer on a 10-millimetre edge quite comfortably, and lock off 1–5–8 on small campus rungs.

What is your favourite finger strength exercise?

If I wanted to work my fingers I would go larger footholds, less steep angle – just over vertical – and small crimps. The kind of holds where you really need to work your fingers and hands to just hold a position.

What is the most common mistake people make when training?

The most common mistake I have seen – and I'm as guilty as anyone else – is overtraining.

JERRY MOFFATT ON *DOMINATOR*, YOSEMITE, USA. © *KURT ALBERT*

Rest and recuperation are vital for building strength. You have to be patient with improvement, nothing goes up on a straight scale – you have to be prepared for the dips.

What is your advice for climbers who want to improve?

Have a goal and write it down. Keep a record of your training. Avoiding injury is key – I would always warm up and stretch. I know it's intense, but I would go to bed and wake up at the same times, as the body likes routine. Eat well – only the best fuel goes into a Formula One car. Finger strength is important because your fingers are your link to the rock, so work hard on that. I would focus on power over endurance because if your power increases your endurance will increase; it doesn't work the other way around. It's harder to get

power, but once you have it you will retain it for longer. Work on your weaknesses. Educate yourself in all things to do with climbing and find a really good coach. Finally, always be mindful of how you convert your training into what you want to achieve.

What are the differences between elite climbers today and elite climbers from your generation?

Elite climbers today have amazing training facilities and it's much easier now to research and find out what other people are doing. Mentally, I think it's the same now as it was for me – you are just trying as hard as you can to climb as well as you can. I was completely obsessed which is what you have to be to reach a very high standard in most things.

You've been the best climber in the world: in your prime, how do you think you would compare against elite climbers today?
It absolutely blows me away how good the top climbers are today. It's unthinkable for me to imagine what people are onsighting and redpointing. I've been lucky to see some very hard stuff redpointed by Alex Megos and Adam Ondra – it was so exhilarating to watch.

In my career, I was very lucky in that when I started it was all very amateur and when I finished there were competitions and you could make a good living from travelling around the world and just going climbing. It was the very best of dreams come true. How would I compare today? I think I would have been good but not the best.

MÉLISSA LA NEVÉ

After a successful competition career which earned her 10 bouldering world cup medals, Mélissa has turned her hand to rock climbing with the same tenacity that we loved watching her compete with. She seems to go out of her way to pick particularly tough challenges, rather than settling for any low-hanging fruit! In 2020, she became the first woman to climb *Action Directe* in the Frankenjura – an amazing ascent as the first move, a huge dyno off a tiny pocket, is renowned for being very hard for shorter people. She has also bouldered 8b+ in Font, climbing *Mécanique Élémentaire*, a horizontal roof with huge moves between pockets.

What is your 5-second maximum one-arm hang on the Beastmaker 2000 middle edge? (How much weight can you add and hang for 5 seconds?)
I mainly hang one arm on the small edge (the outer edges on the Beastmaker 2000) with 2 to 4 kilograms of extra weight depending on my fitness. I never really try to add weight on the middle edge but in comparison I guess I could add probably around 8 to 10kg.

What is your maximum number of one-armers?
Two and a half!

What is your favourite finger strength exercise?
Recently I played a lot designing five-move problems with only my front two fingers and holding them for two seconds before moving.

What is the most common mistake people make when training?
They don't have a proper plan on what to do and why. I see a lot of people trying their hardest hang before even warming up or before doing long hangs to prepare their fingers.

What is your advice for climbers who want to improve?
Fix a goal you want to reach and design a training plan which will help you to get it.

Step by step, preserve your fingers and maximise your abilities. Start with long hangs and then you can start to train more specifically.

TOMOA NARASAKI

Tomoa is one of the best competition climbers out there at the moment. He's won the overall bouldering world cup three times, and has won 20 medals at bouldering and lead world cup events. He's also flashed Font 8b+ (*Decided*, Mizugaki, Japan) on seemingly one of the few times he has bothered to go climbing outside! Climbing looks totally effortless for Tomoa. He's known for his dynamic style, spending more time off the holds than on them, and he seems to be able to jump out of and into the most improbable positions.

What is your favourite finger strength exercise?

Simply climb *kachi* (Japanese word for crimp!) problems and focus on stabilising the body.

What is the most common mistake people make when training?

After trying to reinforce a specific skill or train a body part, it is found that it made the total balance of the body corrupted.

What is your advice for climbers who want to improve?

It's important to focus on your upcoming target or goal. Sometimes you will stop and relax to see your overall environment and body condition; then change your training accordingly. Make sure you are always going in the right direction to become stronger.

ALEX MEGOS

Alex is one of the strongest climbers to walk the earth. He is the first person to onsight F9a (*Estado Critico*, Siurana) and the second person to ever climb a F9c route (*Bibliographie*, Céüse). Coupled with world cup gold medals and multiple Font 8c boulder problems, he is one of the best climbers to ever exist. I have been fortunate to climb and train with Alex a fair bit and what always strikes me is that his drive and tenacity are beyond anything I have ever seen. He absolutely loves training and just doesn't know how to give up!

What is your 5-second maximum one-arm hang on the Beastmaker 2000 middle edge? (How much weight can you add and hang for 5 seconds?)

I once could hang with 25 kilograms of additional weight on the Beastmaker middle edge. With 30 kilograms I did it for 3 seconds, but not for 5.

How long can you hold the Beastmaker six-millimetre micros for (two arms!)?

As long as I need to ;-). Never really tried but I reckon a minute should be no problem and then the tips are probably through ...

What is your maximum number of one-armers?

I think I could never do more than five per arm.

What is your favourite finger strength exercise?

My two favourite fingerboarding exercises are one-arm maximum hangs with additional weight and the 7/3 repeaters for power endurance on the Beastmaker middle edge. I usually do 4x 7/3, then 2 minutes rest and six sets in total.

ALEX MEGOS ON *HUBBLE*, RAVEN TOR, ENGLAND. © *FRANK KRETSCHMANN*

ALEX HONNOLD

What is the most common mistake people make when training?
I think the most common mistake people make when training is that they train their strengths and neglect their weaknesses. People who are powerful train power and people who are technical only climb on vertical walls. It's hard to train something you are not good at, but that's what will make you a better climber in the long run.

What is your advice for climbers who want to improve?
Go climbing! And for the first five years or so don't even bother with specific training. Specific training is the last part of the way to becoming strong. You first need to create the base, and that's for most people getting in some mileage.

Also, more is always more; too much though is not very good at all. Campus boarding does not count as antagonist training and fingerboarding is not a rest day.

Wood is better than resin, and both should be brushed.

Also, hobby bodybuilding and excessive weight lifting are not necessarily beneficial for improvement in climbing.

Carrots for power.

World famous for his free soloing exploits, Alex became the first person to free solo El Capitan when he climbed *Freerider* in 2017. Alex is now a household name and has launched climbing into the public consciousness. He's helped to make it 'cool'! Alex is as bold as it's possible for a human to be, but he's also no slouch at pulling down – having climbed F9a (*Arrested Development*, Mount Charleston)!

What is your 5-second maximum one-arm hang on the Beastmaker 2000 middle edge? (How much weight can you add and hang for 5 seconds?)
I've never been able to hang with one hand. I'm not really sure why because I try my best. But I've never really been closer than minus 10 per cent bodyweight or so.

How long can you hold the Beastmaker six-millimetre micros for (two arms!)?
Not sure if I've ever actually weighted them. I touch them sometimes as a bit of a joke. They feel like hanging off of a butter knife ... I honestly think my fingertips would cut right off.

What is your maximum number of one-armers?
In my life, maybe two and a half?! But in general, I hover around being able to do one but not well.

What is your favourite finger strength exercise?
I think max weighted hangs are my favourite finger exercises, though obviously I could use a lot more of them in my life ... But actually, in my van I normally just use the pre-set

ALEX HONNOLD FINGERBOARDING IN HIS VAN. © *JIMMY CHIN*

Beastmaker repeater workouts just because I can't add weight and they're easy to execute. (Meaning an easy protocol to follow, but they're incredibly hard for me to actually do.)

What is the most common mistake people make when training?

I think that not having a plan is maybe the most common mistake in training. I've spent years 'training', which just meant climbing a lot and getting really tired. But there was no progression to it and no plan – it's definitely not the best way to improve.

What is your advice for climbers who want to improve?

It depends on someone's level. I think for beginner to advanced climbers they can

probably improve the most just by climbing a lot in a variety of styles. But I think for expert/elite climbers it starts to get a lot more complicated to train in an effective way. Well really, I guess it becomes more challenging to find climbs that test them in the appropriate ways. Imagine someone like Alex Megos or Adam Ondra trying to train by only climbing outside – there are only a few routes in the world that are even challenging for them!

I wish I'd started hangboarding and training in a more systematic way at a much younger age. But alas, I grew up in an era where that kind of thing didn't really exist (or at least it didn't at my casual, suburban climbing gym).

SHAUNA COXSEY

My wife! Shauna is known for her competition achievements – 11 world cup gold medals, two overall world cup bouldering titles and one of the first climbers to qualify for our sport's first appearance at the Olympic Games. But she's also totally world class outdoors. With her ascent of *New Base Line* in Magic Wood in 2014, she became only the third woman in the world to climb Font 8b+ and she has climbed loads of other hard stuff around the world on our travels. Of course, I'm more proud of her than I could ever put into words, even though she leaves the toilet seat down …

What is your 5-second maximum one-arm hang on the Beastmaker 2000 middle edge? (How much weight can you add and hang for 5 seconds?)
I think my max was around 15 kilograms. Which kinda blows my mind now as body weight feels hard enough these days.

How long can you hold the Beastmaker six-millimetre micros for (two arms!)?
I have no idea. I am not a fan of being uncomfortable – they are just too gross for me!

What is your maximum number of one-armers?
I once did three in a row. But for me they are so random. Some days I can do them and other days I can't. I find my ability to do a one-armer has no bearing on my ability to climb well.

What is your favourite finger strength exercise?
Max hangs for sure. Although I use them for more of a maintenance session than full max. I generally do one 2-arm and one 1-arm session a week.

What is the most common mistake people make when training?
Forgetting that climbing is about climbing. Getting strong takes dedication and patience but getting good at climbing takes so much more than that. From technical intricacies to the psychological demands, climbing requires a plethora of skills that are not only hard to train but they are personal, specific to the individual and you can't simply read a book to get better at them. Luckily you can read this book and learn how to get strong so at least that's one thing sorted!

What is your advice for climbers who want to improve?
Set yourself some goals. Specific to you and achievable. Big goals, little goals. Remember these when you're training. And find ways to smile always.

SHAUNA COXSEY ON *MERLIN'S BEARD*, TINTAGEL, ENGLAND. © *NED FEEHALLY*

FREQUENTLY ASKED QUESTIONS

HOW SHOULD I WARM UP?

NF: It's a good idea to figure out your own warm-up routine. Everyone is different, so there isn't a one-warm-up-fits-all approach. Personally, I climb best when I know my fingers are warm and ready to pull as hard as possible, and also when my body has been moving a bit. Only warming up my fingers and then jumping straight on the rocks/wall will leave me feeling like a clumsy oaf. I like to do a bit of moving and a bit of stretching, followed by some finger-specific warming up on a fingerboard. After this I begin to climb, generally starting on pretty easy and low-angled terrain and progressing on to steeper and harder climbing. Of course, if I'm warming up for a slab problem, the process will be a little different to if I'm warming up to climb in a roof!

> **SC:** I think climbers often don't value warming up enough. I use my warm-up as a way to check in with my body. My warm-up routine is a mini mobility, conditioning and fingerboard routine that acts as everyday maintenance. I generally spend at least an hour warming up.

HOW OFTEN SHOULD I FINGERBOARD?

While fingerboarding alone won't make you a better climber, having more finger strength is always a good thing! The most important aspect of finger strength training is consistency over many years. Fingerboarding once a week for three years will do you more good than fingerboarding five times a week for two months and then stopping all together.

Fitting in a short but intense fingerboard session is fairly time efficient and it shouldn't leave you feeling too tired. So, I think you can easily fingerboard two or three times a week (once you have worked up to it, of course) and climb on top of that.

> Fingerboarding is one of the foundations of my training. I usually do two fingerboard sessions a week, primarily for maintaining strength but I also think fingerboarding helps with injury prevention.

I DON'T WANT TO RUIN MY CLIMBING SESSION BY FEELING TIRED, SO WHEN SHOULD I FINGERBOARD?

Always train strength and power *before* other forms of training. Fingerboarding is strength training and so should be performed when you are most fresh.

Over time you will adapt to your fingerboard sessions. I usually fingerboard first, and then climb a few hours later. Even when I'm heading out rock climbing, I like to do a fingerboard warm-up first so I can gauge how I'm feeling. It takes time to get into it, but I find it very useful.

But, of course, if you plan to climb after your fingerboard session, you should focus on shorter, more intense hangs on the fingerboard, rather than diving into a hardcore power endurance workout. This will mean you are minimally fatigued for your second session, but you've still given your body a good stimulus to adapt to. For me, a warm-up and three max hangs in a full crimp position prepares me well and doesn't wear me out for my climbing session.

MARTIN SMITH ON *LA BALEINE*, ROCHER CANON, FONTAINEBLEAU, FRANCE. © *NICK BROWN*

I love to use the fingerboard as a warm-up for climbing sessions. It took me a while to build up to this routine, but now it works really well.

HOW MANY FINGERBOARD SESSIONS SHOULD I DO TO TRAIN A GRIP TYPE BEFORE GOING ON TO TRAIN ANOTHER?

I usually train different grip types during different sessions in a typical week. So, I might do a couple of full crimp sessions, a half crimp session and an open hand session all within one week. This keeps things interesting and makes sure my body is constantly having to adapt to different stimuli.

I've found that I need to do at least 10 sessions of a particular fingerboard exercise to make and consolidate any gains. This means that after five to 10 weeks I'd look at mixing up that particular session. Of course, if I felt like I was still making progress with that grip type, I'd stick with it until progress began to plateau, and then I'd move on to something else.

In essence, if it's working, keep doing it! Only change your methods when your existing system no longer seems to be producing any results.

SHOULD I TRAIN FULL CRIMPED?
In short: yes, definitely.

In my experience it makes sense to train full crimped. Not training your full crimp and then expecting it to perform when you need it is a bit daft. Full crimping is really useful on steep ground as it allows you to get into the back of holds and pull inwards as well as downwards, which gives you way more control throughout a move.

I always train crimping on the fingerboard without my thumbs (but with all fingers in the flexed position), as I find that using the thumbs can tear my cuticles. Crimping without thumbs transfers well to crimping with thumbs as the fingers are at the same angles.

> So, I'm naturally a half crimper and I rarely train full crimped. I have never found that my full crimp is weak and so I haven't felt the need to train it. I think this is because the majority of the climbing I do is indoors where the holds don't really get that small and gnarly. For all-round climbing, however, or on particular rock types, being able to full crimp is essential and you should train it if it's a weakness.

DO I NEED TO BE ABLE TO DO A ONE-ARMER TO BE GOOD AT CLIMBING?
Absolutely not! Being strong and being good often get confused. Being a good climber encompasses all sorts of technical, tactical and strength-based skills. Having the strength to do a one-armer can be very useful, *provided* you have the climbing skills to put that strength to good use.

> Definitely not! One-armers are so random – on some days I can't do one and other days I can do three in a row. They're a great party trick but not at all essential for climbing hard.

HOW CAN I BREAK A PLATEAU?
Generally, you'll plateau when you do the same thing for a long time without any changes. So, changing the stimulus on your body will kick-start a process of improvement. For a lot of climbers, this is as simple as going climbing more. If you climb two or three times a week, then try going more often. Other climbers may need to change what they are climbing on – it might be that you need to try harder on more difficult climbs. Or you could introduce some specific finger strength training. A lot of advanced climbers could make huge gains by stretching more and by learning to climb with the increased flexibility and mobility this would create!

> I think variety is the secret to avoiding both physical and mental plateaus. Changing things is so important, whether it's doing different exercises or climbing in different places.